LONDON

LONDON
BREAD AND CIRCUSES

JONATHAN GLANCEY

VERSO

London • New York

First published by Verso 2001
© Jonathan Glancey 2001
All photographs © Nigel Fowler Sutton, except those listed on p.148
All rights reserved

The moral rights of the author have been asserted

1 3 5 7 9 10 8 6 4 2

Verso
UK: 6 Meard Street, London W1F 0EG
USA: 180 Varick Street, New York, NY 10014–4606
www.versobooks.com

Verso is the imprint of New Left Books

ISBN 1–85984–645–9

British Library Cataloguing in Publication Data
A catalogue record for this book is available from the British Library

Library of Congress Cataloging-in-Publication Data
A catalog record for this book is available from the Library of Congress

Printed by Biddles Ltd, Guildford and King's Lynn
www.biddles.co.uk

In memory of Frank Pick
(1878–1941)

Old Father Chaos in these wild Spaces reigns absolute and upholds his Realms of Darkness. He presses hard upon our frontier ...

ANTHONY ASHLEY COOPER, THE MORALISTS, 1709

BREAD
AND
CIRCUSES

I n spring 2001, I witnessed two London events within a week: the May Day demonstration culminating at Oxford Circus, and Tracey Emin's "opening" at the White Cube Gallery, Hoxton Square.

The first represented the rump of the London Mob, inheritors of those who have risen up over the centuries to reclaim the streets for the interests of the "people". In June 1381 a Mob led by Wat Tyler, Jack Straw and John Ball mingled with eastern county rebels drawn from Norfolk down to Kent to fight a hated poll tax being collected by corrupt officials to pay for England's wars with France. The Mob broke open prisons, burned public records, tipped the contents of John of Gaunt's Savoy Palace into the Thames, beheaded lawyers and torched the great Hospital of the Knights Templar. At Smithfield it met its match in Richard II. The teenage king offered to be its champion and led the crowd to the fields of Clerkenwell. Wat Tyler was cut down by William Walworth, Lord Mayor of London, outside the future St Bartholomew's Hospital. Promised beer and freedom from arrest by the young king – the fourteenth-century equivalent of bread and circuses – the Mob dispersed.

It re-emerged in various guises, in 1414 at the time of the Lollard Revolt and to support Jack Cade's uprising in 1450. It rose again on Evil May Day 1517, when the London apprentices rioted. And again at the time of the Wilkes Riots of 1768 which ended with troops opening fire on the crowd at St George's Fields. It was at its most anarchistic during the anti-Catholic and anti-Irish Gordon Riots of June 1780. A crowd, fifty thousand strong, stormed across the Thames from St George's Fields, Southwark, torched five prisons, and, hideously drunk on looted gin, wine and beer, indulged in an orgy of death and destruction. By the next morning, the 3rd of June, 850 people lay dead. Twenty-one ringleaders were executed.

There have been many great political demonstrations in London since, among them the Spitalfields Riots of 1816, the Clerkenwell Riots of 1832 and those in Trafalgar Square in 1848, 1886 and 1887 ("Bloody Sunday"). More recently there have been the anti-Vietnam student demonstrations of the mid-1960s which culminated in the Grosvenor Square riots of 1967–68, and the arrival of punk in the late 1970s. Race riots were a general feature of the second half of the twentieth century – Notting Hill in 1958, Brixton in 1981 and Tottenham in 1985, when PC Blakelock was murdered at Broadwater Farm, a run-down council estate. And of course there was the twentieth-century equivalent of the 1381 riot when protesters forced Margaret Thatcher's Tory government to abandon a new poll tax in 1990 after a memorable battle with the forces of law and order also in Trafalgar Square. Modern politicians, it appeared, had no sense of history, which has, as Karl Marx reminds us, that tricky habit of repeating itself first as tragedy and then as farce.

The Reclaim the Streets and anti-globalisation marches of the past decade revived fears of the London Mob and of the Clash's White Riot. Yet, what a pitiful sight the New Mob made on the 1st of May 2001: a small gang of what tabloid newspapers dubbed "rioters" hemmed into London's retail core by a phalanx of armoured police at Oxford Circus. Heroism and heckling evaporated as the modern-day blue-uniformed legionaries refused to budge and the need to go to the lavatory (of which there are precious few on the streets of London) weakened the spirit of latter-day Wat Tylers, John Balls and Jack Straws.

In 1381, the Mob, which was drawn mostly from the peasantry and would have pissed on the spot, had marched to the chant

When Adam delved, and Eve span
Who was then a gentleman?

In 2001, the New Mob was made up mostly of gentlefolk, university-educated, middle-class men and women. Six hundred years down the line from the Peasants' Revolt and just over a decade on from the Thatcher poll-tax riot, it seemed a rather harmless, carefree gathering. But at root there was a genuine anger about how London has gone the way of all global cities, falling prey to the carrier-bag clutches of mass retail culture, its perfidious brands, infernal logos and the cheap labour it employs to keep Londoners in the kind of leisurewear both protesters and politicians wear when they take to the streets.

Demonstrations and riots are the extreme end of political debate. They can be messy and even deadly events. They may or may not achieve their goals. But they are almost always a last resort, the only response left when people feel that those in power have failed to listen to the tide of public opinion. Of course there will always be some people who just want a fight or love the sound of breaking glass, but there is also a growing crowd of popular dissenters who believe that life means a lot more than shopping, holidays, brands, networking, clubbing and watching television, and who believe too that governments, especially those of a Labour stripe, should be more than mere mouthpieces for big business and the interests of a well-heeled minority.

What has happened to radical politics in London as we enter the twenty-first century? To a city which once hosted not only Mobs but also a young Vladimir Illych Lenin, who edited *Iskra* (the Spark) from an office on Clerkenwell Green and used to drink at The Crown Tavern? To answer that we need to go back twenty years or so. London lost much of its skilled and politically active workforce in the 1980s, when dockers, printers and transport workers were largely disbanded or tamed. In exchange, as it were, for their political consciousness,

Mrs Thatcher's governments offered the working class a stake in the free-market economy: the sale of council homes and a share in the newly privatised public utilities. Now everyone from Upminster to Uxbridge, Stanmore to Streatham could be a capitalist. At the same time, a consumer boom changed the face of London's high streets, the tone of the media and people's aspirations. Greed was good and shopping was truly the new religion; Brent Cross, Lakeside and, latterly, Bluewater its temples. Serious news reporting and features were increasingly squeezed out of newspapers and magazines in favour of shopping and shopping-related stories. Food. Fashion. Restaurants. Interior décor. Garden makeovers. As Londoners snuffed their noses into this deepening trough, the Tories wallowed in sleaze.

The New Labour government of Tony Blair might have been expected to sweep a clean broom through this consumerist swill. But it didn't. Instead it offered a more ambitious form of "designer" Thatcherism (all that "Cool Britannia" nonsense) and played on a nation's desire to get rich quick with the Lottery. It offered its own versions of the Colosseum (the Dome), and the theatres and circuses of Ancient Rome (the Millennium projects that are dotted through this book). It did this with one hand, while the other continued to strip London's public sector of any pride and independence it might once have had with dogmatic free-market policies that saw privatisation move silently and stealthily through the city like the sleekest sewer rat.

It's hard to avoid the suspicion that Londoners are being bought off by New Labour with dashing architecture, modish cafes and sumptuous museums. Attractive additions to the city though these may be, they start to look like a shoddy exercise in the promotion of passivity when set alongside the state of London's transport, schools and hospitals. It's as if, no matter how bad things get – and we all know they're really bad – we'll be happily distracted by the chance to shop, eat and view art in a few gorgeous buildings. And perhaps many of us are – even when Londoners had a chance in the summer of 2001 to protest against the folly of breaking up the Underground and hiving parts of it off to private enterprise, only a handful turned up at the Law Courts in the Strand to protest.

Any sort of radicalism, it seems, is something confined very definitely to the past. Who is willing now to engage in serious and patient discussion about the way London is run, or fails to run? Who, outside a small coterie of critics and academics, wants to talk about rather slow and dogged things like justice, the public good, public administration, planning or the "common wealth" – the "common treasury" as Gerald Winstanley and the Diggers put it – when there are ever more opportunities to shop, eat, drink, do drugs, worry about mortgages, watch tv and dance? Or hang out at happening art events.

Our scene changes to Hoxton, 'orrible 'Oxton of only a decade ago when gangs of thugs still roamed its seemingly unchartered streets. But that was then and this was April 2001. Tracey Emin, the media's artist-of-the-moment, was enjoying the opening of her latest show at the fashionable cockney outpost of the svelte St James's White Cube Gallery. Hoxton Square was packed. My dears, you should have seen the crush. Tout Londres was there, m'wah m'wahing for New Britain. Gleaming young things trying out their fledgling Mockney, or having a bash at the New Cries of London … "I was, like, fuck off" … Artful authors unveiling their latest arcane simile with the wry arch of just the one eyebrow. Broadsheet editors who would have been happier at Arsenal or the Groucho Club. A matt black of tv producers, a cool knowingness of arty-smarties, a free-beeriness of professional students. And me.

This, I couldn't help thinking, was the apotheosis of New London and its New Mob, splashing happily in a tide of sponsored booze, cute art, fashion, the "creative industries" and the approval of media, government and police. At that moment, all over central London, other representatives of the New Mob were out late-night shopping for designer labels along teeming Oxford Street. Shuffling through the "accessible", Department-of-Culture-approved galleries of the Tate Modern. Riding the London Eye. Trawling the encyclopaedic pages of Time Out for the best of this week's new sushi bars, or night-clubs with an ironic Seventies' revival edge. Finding their way by studying new City of Westminster street signs sponsored by HSBC (in prominent letters). Making the all-important choice between tall, family and unfeasibly large cups of weak, muddy, West Coast coffee in chain cafes run by the latest wave of smiling, low-wage immigrants.

In a transcendental moment, I felt as if I was rising like some cockney sparrow or the spirit of William Blake and, looking down on my own city – one of the world's greatest – saw it boozing and shopping away its political consciousness as it bopped to the tune of a thousand advertising jingles. Two thousand years flashed before my eyes and I was standing in Londinium alongside a supercilious legate from Rome in a purple-edged toga. "Bread and circuses", he sneered. And, with that, I was transported back to Hoxton Square with his words ringing in my ears.

Rome reached its zenith in about 200AD. The population had peaked at about 1.25 million, crowded into a labyrinth of canyon-like streets busy with traffic and commerce twenty-four hours a day. Two centuries earlier Julius Caesar had complained of the incessant noise that stopped him sleeping, but Rome in 200AD was a much busier place. The imperial hub, this teeming cosmopolitan metropolis was home to freemen and slaves of every creed and colour. Most rented jerry-built apartments in blocks of concrete flats, some up to eight storeys high (as close to the gods as any city dweller was expected to live before the advent of Mr Otis's lift in the 1850s). Public transport was inadequate. Traffic jams were endemic. Sounds familiar?

And yet in the midst of this sword-and-sandal chaos were some of the greatest buildings the world had seen. Here was the Forum with its bombastic temples and voluminous basilicas, its court houses and trading floors. Here were public baths built on the scale of the most ambitious nineteenth-century railway stations and fed by stupendous aqueducts. Over there, the Pantheon with its gold-leafed dome, a paean to the latest construction technology, and the Emperor Hadrian's representation of the Universe. There, the Circus Maximus, Trajan's Market and, most dramatic of all, the Colosseum. In these costly monuments, predecessors as I've suggested of the Millennium follies London has invested in so headily over the past five years, the Romans were fed an exchequer-draining diet of bread and circuses.

The idea was simple. To keep the "plebs" in order, all that was needed was entertainment on an epic scale. And the Romans, who have since fed Hollywood's ravenous appetite for blockbusters, understood the dramatic, populist gesture better than any civilisation before or since, including Hitler's Germany, Roosevelt's USA, Stalin's Soviet Union, and, inevitably, Tony Blair's cool, millennial New Britain.

Yet, as with Rome, so with London. The best way to keep the people in order and to stop them thinking practically about serious issues is to keep them entertained. As recently as 1868, London still boasted Colosseum-style entertainment in the guise of public executions held at Tyburn, Smithfield and Newgate. These had long been crowd-pleasers, but reached a peak in Regency London when crowds of between 100,000 and 200,000 tipped up for celebrity executions. The last beheading at the Tower of London was that of the Jacobite Lord Lovat who, just before the axe fell, smiled to see a grandstand collapse killing twelve of the richer ghouls who had paid through the nose to get a good look at his judicial murder. The last beheadings of all took place outside Newgate (demolished in 1902 and replaced by the Old Bailey) in 1820. The crowd howled with pleasure as a gang of latter-day Guy Fawkes had their heads parted slowly from their shoulders with a surgeon's knife. The executioner accidentally dropped the last head; the crowd, always game for a laugh, shouted "Butterfingers!"

Public executions stopped not because of a sudden wave of altruism washing over government and judiciary, but because they generated crime and mayhem on an epic scale. When a pieman fell over at the execution of Holloway and Haggerty in 1807, the crowd panicked and nearly a hundred people died. Once, according to the London diarist Samuel Pepys, when a prisoner was reprieved at the last moment, the indignant crowd ripped up the profitable seats – stalls and grandstands – and a riot ensued. "It was a ribald, reckless, brutal mob, violently combative . . . fiercely aggressive, distinctly abusive", Pepys wrote. (London Encyclopaedia)

What could be done to entertain people now that executions were held in private, only for the privileged few to leer at? The answer, for some at least, was football, association football, which emerged soon after the ban on public executions. The crowds could be contained, more or less safely, by the Metropolitan Police (founded in 1829) inside a new generation of mini-Colossea (Fulham, opened in 1879; Orient, 1881; Tottenham Hotspur, 1882; Queen's Park Rangers, 1885; Millwall, 1885; Arsenal, 1886). Even then, they could get ugly, as they did in 1923 at the first FA Cup Final to be played in the new Wembley Stadium, between Bolton and West Ham.

But in truth professional football developed fairly slowly, with attendance not building up to 40,000 or more until the turn of the century and crowds generally behaving remarkably well. It wasn't until the 1980s, when the British Movement attempted to win over the dimmer lights among London crowds, that football hooliganism reached an all-time high. Mrs Thatcher, the prime minister, was all for introducing identity cards to keep a tag on the crowds, but this was widely seen as an infringement of civil liberties. She diverted her energies instead to the Falkland Islands, a circus in the guise of a real-life war drama – the age-old way of turning the public's attention away from home-spun problems like unemployment, public-sector emasculation and a collapsing industrial base.

Since then, association football in London has become the deeply fashionable plaything of the middle classes. Chelsea FC boasts a Las Vegas-style shopping mall; a ten-year lease on an executive box here costs £1 million. Arsenal FC, meanwhile, is planning to redevelop both its handsome Art Deco stadium and the cosy terraced streets around it. Soon enough, a new generation of local lads and ladettes will be enjoying post-match sushi parties in Piers Gough-designed lofts and apartments, one league up from those flanking the Tate Modern in fashionable Southwark.

Not that Tate Modern has much to worry about – it is one of the jewels in New Labour's bread and circuses crown. A big, populist art project, it is the most successful of the Millennium shows provided for Londoners and visitors to the capital not least because it lured 5.5 million people through its mighty portals in its first twelve months. This was nearly three times the target it had set itself and not so very far behind the number of visitors to the long-established British

Museum (7 million in 2000). But Tate Modern on a Sunday after-noon is a heady cocktail of shopping mall, stadium and art gallery. You would never come here to relax or to contemplate works of art. If you wanted to do that, you would head upriver to Tate Britain (1897), built on the site of Millbank Penitentiary, whose displays of English paintings include those of the peerless cockney artists Hogarth (born in Smithfield in 1697), Blake (Soho, 1757) and Turner (Soho, 1775).

London's shops, meanwhile, have turned themselves into mass-appeal galleries in which the contemporary art and design they display so enticingly is very much for sale. The Conran Shop on Fulham Road, for instance, stocked with designer goodies and trin-kets, bears a striking resemblance to Terence Conran's Design Museum at Butler's Wharf. The only real difference is that the objects on display at the Conran Shop carry price tags while those at the Design Museum don't. Where Culture seemed somehow superior to or simply snootier than Commerce in the days when bodies like the Arts Council and Design Council had something to say, the two have dovetailed almost seamlessly together over the past twenty years. As with Ancient Rome, so with New London ...

One of the difficulties in avoiding New Labour's bread and circuses show is that London, more than any other European city (except perhaps post-Soviet Moscow), has prostrated itself on the altar of free enterprise. It offers a bewildering and ever-increasing choice of goods, services and ways of life to the free-market faithful. The laws of the market are invoked to enable us to satisfy our apparently insa-tiable and urgent demand for whatever we want whenever we want it. A soggy, lukewarm burger in a nursery-coloured polystyrene box eaten on an overlit Tube train. The right to annoy fellow passengers ("customers" in free-market speak) with the insistent tss-tss-tss of a sod-you personal stereo. A pizza big enough to feed a family of six delivered to your flat by a teenager barely able to ride the bald-tyred moped he needs to reach you before your 3,000-calorie video snack gets cold. Unprotected sex with eastern Europeans on the make for a few quid just a piss-streaked telephone-kiosk's call away.

Such freedom of choice is the crude, if effective, philosophical underpinning of New London. It encourages a society in which people scream ever more loudly to be heard like starlings gathered in autumn swarms in Leicester Square. It is an echo of Mrs Thatcher's great contribution to moral philosophy: "There is no such thing as society. There are individual men and women and families." It is atavism played out on a metropolitan scale. It is the antithesis of the old London County Council's stuffy, patronising, intelligent-design-and-decent-public-services-are-good-for-you approach when London was run by socialists and liberals, and red school exercise books were emblazoned with the LCC crest. It is quite probably the reason why London's workforce has become ever less skilled and why the divide between rich and poor has grown as almost never before.

Low paid, unskilled work is one of the keys to London's "success". The much-talked-about freedom of choice we are all meant to enjoy so much today – the longer opening hours, the eat-and-drink-what-you-want-when-you-want-it city – are possible only because of cheap, hidden and even illegal labour. Many of the jobs the service industries rely on to survive are unpalatable to Londoners – the work is seen as demeaning and exploitative – and, as in that other site of unbridled free-market economics, the USA, it is the city's immigrants who most often fill the breach. The purist free-marketeers would argue that by keeping wages and union interference low we are able not only to increase the number and variety of services on offer in London, but to offer work to those fleeing from tyranny and poverty abroad. (Ultra-capitalism is moral after all.)

When I travel to those parts of London black cabs don't like to go (especially north-of-the-river men) I find myself involved in conversations with mini-cab drivers such as the trainee accountant from Afghanistan who had fought the Russians in hand-to-hand combat, the Bangladeshi setting up in the rag trade who hadn't as yet been able to persuade his beautiful young bride to give up downtown Dacca for suburban Wembley, and the angry Bosnian who gave me an insider's low-down on why everyone else in former Yugoslavia deserves to die slowly and painfully. Surely not everyone, I asked, as a livid cyclist cut us up and gave us a V-sign. "My friend, you don't understand; these people are animals . . ." This all makes a change from the near-statutory black-cab conversation about golfing holidays in Florida, gambling holidays in Las Vegas and how Ken Livingstone is a waste of space. "What's he done for London?" asks a Pringle-sweatered cabbie accusingly as we launch down Piccadilly in a tropical downpour past the long queue of tourists outside the Hard Rock Cafe. "I'll tell you for free what Ken Livingstone's done for London," he says as the meter clocks up another 20 pence, "fucking nothing . . ."

Nothing comes of nothing. We depend for our cleaners, drivers, nurses, sandwich-bar and shop assistants on cheap immigrant labour. Where would be without them? What, in any case, would London be like without the waves of immigrants who have washed up against her mud banks and marshes? The city was, after all, founded by Italians and knocked into shape over the centuries under a ruling class and monarchies which have been variously Roman, Romano-British, Anglo-Saxon (German Vikings), Norman (Frenchified

Vikings), Welsh (Tudors), Scottish (Stuarts), Dutch (William and Mary), German again (Hanoverians, Saxe-Coburgs, Windsors); all of these were interbred with Spaniards, Greeks and doubtless many others besides. Its workforce has been drawn over the past three centuries from Huguenots escaping persecution in France following the Revocation of the Edict of Nantes in 1685 and bringing their fine silk-weaving skills to the factious, non-conformist streets of Spitalfields, to Irish navvies escaping the potato famine of 1846, to Russian Jews, Italians, Poles, Indians, West Indians, Caribbeans, Afro-Caribbeans, Greek Cypriots, Somalis, Bosnians, Kurds, Romanians . . . each has brought London something new and, over time, has found its place and purpose. Without them, and without today's immigrants who help to sustain the way London functions, our lives would be economically and culturally much poorer.

Reminders of London's immigrant populations abound – in the names of streets, pubs and banks, and perhaps most obviously in its eating establishments (the Lahore Kebab House in the East End, for instance; coffee bars and cafes like Soho's Bar Italia and Maison Bertaux). But so much else about the city is transient, forever changing. What happened to the Greek working mens' cafe on Tottenham Street, for instance? It used to boast the biggest cat in London, although it had a rival, the possibly even bigger cat that, if you asked nicely and the coast was clear, you could see inside the ladies' lavatory at Paddington station. Or the shop in Bloomsbury where old ladies sold hand-knitted cardies until recently? Where did Jules Bar on Jermyn Street go with its signed RAF photos, leggy blondes, blue lagoon cocktails and School-of-Terry-Thomas-meets-Leslie-Phillips floorwalkers? Or Chiswick Bus Works? Or old Covent Garden market? Where's Gamages with its magical toy department, or Whitechapel Baths? Why is Richard Harris having to close his impeccable Bloomsbury car repair and engineering workshop and move out of London? What happened to the original Pavilion restaurant, a Festival of Britain fantasmagoria designed by Angus McBean who had photographed a young Vivien Leigh in London? Gone with the wind. London consumes itself much like the mythical serpent that appears to be eating its own tail in a quest for perpetual renewal.

London's residents are similar: whenever they make a bit of money, they move. They always have, from self-made Roman London merchants investing in centrally heated Kentish villas to Mr Pooter, a celebrated fictional Victorian nobody moving his clerkish family to the Laurels, Holloway Road, which seemed oh so respectable a century ago. In the 1930s Londoners emigrated to mock-Tudor Metroland. In the Fifties, to the new towns – Stevenage, Crawley, Hemel Hempstead – which mopped up what was known as the London "overspill". Later on, it was out along the old A12 or A13 to Essex or down through the Elephant for the last time to a new house at the end of a cul-de-sac with double glazing and a double garage somewhere not that far from Maidstone, and close to a golf course. The middle classes moved too, to ever-further-flung suburbia, to the golf courses, stables and tennis clubs of Hertfordshire, Berkshire, Buckinghamshire, Surrey and Kent, yet still attached by umbilical chords of Tarmac and track to jobs in London.

At one time, before central London living became fashionable, and then profitable for developers and housebuilders in the 1980s, it seemed as if the rich, those living on old money and trust funds, the bohemian, the mad, the newly immigrant and the hopelessly poor had central London to themselves. Of course they had to share it with visitors from overseas as Tourist London began to emerge strongly after the successful Swinging London media whirl of the mid-Sixties. The Bonzo Dog Doo Dah Band teased this with their song "Cool

Britannia" in 1966. The tourists came in their millions. Today they all too often occupy a strange parallel London made up of drab restaurants and shabby shops, looking shocked at the expense of Tube tickets and museum admissions. I think Londoners feel sorry for them, but, as they rarely meet them, there's not much chance to say so. It's hard to explain to a tourist who is likely to spend a holiday in London meeting other tourists that Londoners dart in and out, through, up, over and under their city like rats on speed trying to get out of a trap. London is continually on the move, morphing like a character in a computer game, as restless as a tiger in Regent's Park Zoo and always alert to the next business opportunity. It's rather as if Londoners are all like Patrick McGoohan's Prisoner, who shouted defiantly from the tv screen, "I will not be pushed, filed, stamped, indexed, briefed, debriefed or numbered. My life is my own. I am not a number, I am a free man." So busy are we being free and refusing to be pushed into neat boxes by governments, planners, civil servants and architects that our world, our big, jumbly market stall, runs through our hands like so much soft sand. Soft-sift in an hour glass.

But when was London not in thrall to all-encompassing commerce? How often has it been truly big spirited and possessed of a real desire to sort out its messy infrastructure, its wobbly public services or to help its poor? London was born a trading centre, and whatever cultural ambitions it might have had, or has, it remains essentially a swashbuckling, piratical city buccaneering the high, jolly-rogered seas of commerce. There has been so much talk, especially since the Blitz, of how London can be, must be, planned and ordered; but when has this ever really mattered to a city that at its best and worst is really nothing more, and nothing less, than a giant, colourful, grasping and pugnacious street market? In that question beats the heart of this book.

Roman London, founded in AD43 (and refounded in AD60 after Boadicea, Queen of the Iceni, and her East Anglian Mob razed it to the ground), was not some ideal Classical arcadia, but a smaller version of Rome itself. It boasted an impressive basilica (about the size of St Paul's Cathedral) and other fine public buildings. It would have been cosmopolitan: merchants from North Africa, the Middle East and all parts of western Europe probably came this way. Africans may well have walked the tessellated pavements deep beneath our feet two thousand years ago. Whatever it was like, Roman London was dedicated primarily to the gods of trade and commerce. Writing at the time of Boadicea's raid, Tacitus tells us that Londinium "was not dignified by the title of a colonia [like the much grander Colchester, for example], but was packed with traders and a celebrated centre of commerce". And that, for better or worse, is what it stayed.

The one time London might have reinvented itself as a regular classical city, one in which culture would lead and commerce follow, was, famously, in the aftermath of the Great Fire of London of 1666. Sir Christopher Wren, among others, drew up a handsome, rational plan for the reconstruction of the charred city. It was quickly dismissed. London wanted to get back to the business of making money. Its god was Mammon, who inspired Londoners to rebuild their city along higgledy-piggledy medieval lines and, even though new buildings have grown progressively taller and more substantial than they once were, this venerable street pattern survives. So, too, the names of streets that express London's role as a market: Poultry, Bread Street, Milk Street, Fish Street Hill, Cornhill and Cloth Fair. A market both in terms of goods and financial services: Lombard Street got its name early on from the medieval Italian bankers who came here to help make the City of London the world's most successful financial trading centre which it remains today. And even now the money markets of the City squat cheek by jowl with the meat markets of Smithfield – where hung, drawn and quartered cattle and the odd pig's head are traded – and the cavernous nightclubs that thump away all night long.

True, the medieval London skyline was dominated by churches, monasteries, priories and chapels, but many of London's religious buildings were part and parcel of its commercial life, the focal points of its guilds, crafts and trades. It's true too that from the late seventeenth century a new London began to emerge with the elegant residential squares of Mayfair and Soho. But many of these were built by property developers who spurred on the handsome yet ruthlessly commercial octopus-like spread of London in the eighteenth century, at the end of which the city's population finally topped that of second-century Rome. You have only to look at Hogarth's "The Times of Day" cycle (1738) or "Gin Lane" (1751) to see how dismal life was for the majority of Londoners at the very same time that the fashionable new West End was emerging in cool, Palladian splendour. Of course, this being London, many of the new houses that looked so fine from the outside were shabbily built. Many collapsed before they were completed. That so many survive is testimony to their enduring beauty and, above all, to their adaptability; in recent decades most have been rebuilt to become offices, shops, restaurants and occasionally even homes.

When the Victorians got to work, the face of London changed for ever. They did three key things to the fabric of the city. They connected the City to Westminster and the West End convincingly. They drove their changes through with efficacious public works. And they brought the railways (Bermondsey and London Bridge stations opened in 1836, the year before Victoria came to the throne; most of the rest were complete by 1874). Masters of the insensitive grand project, the Victorians removed vast tracts of slum housing, replacing them with the likes of Liverpool Street and St Pancras stations. They drove Holborn Viaduct through and across the Fleet Valley. They raised fairy-tale buildings like the Palace of Westminster, the Law Courts and the Grand Midland Hotel. They embanked the Thames and constructed the magnificent mains-sewer system that London relies on still to carry its prodigious effluence out to the outfall works at Barking Creek and Crossness. They cut-and-covered the first under-ground railway (Paddington to Farringdon, in 1863). They laid out squares and public parks, invested in conspicuous hospitals and effective street lamps, laid tram tracks, threw a cat's cradle of bridges across the Thames, opened music halls, weighed themselves down with museums draped in shiny terracotta, pricked the skyline with spiky Gothic churches, educated their young in stern, red-brick schools, relocated principal markets, and buried their dead in vast municipal cemeteries (more than half a million Londoners are buried around the nine miles of pathways in the city's biggest, the City of London Cemetery, at Manor Park, built in 1856).

The Victorians also indulged London with grandiloquent head-quarters for learned societies and eager new professions. In 1829 they established the Metropolitan Police and ran the city's first bus service. They soaked the city in a sea of gin palaces, all cut glass, plush, privacy screens and mirrors. They built magnificent public lavatories of a scale, frequency and splendour that make today's efforts look pitiful. They reformed local government, set up the Metropolitan Board of Works in 1855, and its successor, the highly effective LCC, thirty-three years later. And they built the suburbs, those inter-

minable chains of dreary stock-brick houses, some flat-fronted, some
with bay windows, that stretched along the railway lines, ambushed
the pretty old villages of Hampstead, Highgate and Chelsea and
pushed out as far as any Londoner's eye could see from the top of
St Paul's, prompting this refrain in a popular music hall song:

> With a ladder and some glasses
> You could see to Hackney marshes
> If it wasn't for the houses in between

The London we experience today is essentially a heavy-duty and
enduring Victorian overlay on pretty, if flimsy, Georgian foundations
stretched over a medieval street pattern settled (to the east) on
Roman foundations. The result is a mix as rich as that of a figgy
pudding or a bowl of eighteenth-century chocolate supped at
Jonathan's or Child's. In classical or European urban-planning terms,
it's a mess – pragmatic, ruthless, more quirky than beautiful – yet it's
an endlessly intriguing, utterly fascinating, enervating and creative
place to live and work, assuming you can afford to live here in the
first place.

And there's the rub. London's very success, its immense creativity,
particularly in the financial sector, and its exponential physical
growth have made it a city with two enduring problems – it is very
(and increasingly) expensive to live in and it is extremely difficult to
plan and manage.

There was a plan, of sorts, dreamed up after the old London docks
fell into decline and disuse in the 1960s and '70s, to remodel the
whole of the Docklands and to shift the city eastwards along the

Thames. It made sense for a moment. All that disused land. A chance to build a post-modern Jerusalem under the auspices of the energetic London Docklands Development Corporation. It didn't quite work out that way. Instead of all that riverside activity, its thieving docks, ships from all parts of the world, the huge, hairy spiders that crept out of banana boxes, the City of London wharves further upriver with their early-morning smelly barrows and baskets resting alongside Wren churches, the finny thrill of Billingsgate Market (closed in 1982) and Mr Monty chopping eels for Tubby Isaacs on Lovat Lane . . . Instead of these we have the chic and suited banality of Canary Wharf, the cheap clatter-past of the Docklands Light Railway, more boring post-Modern apartment blocks than you care to imagine, and a City riverside as lifeless and as appealing as an empty fridge dumped in Barking Creek.

I miss this part of the City and the eastward stretch of the Thames very much, as I do the Clerkenwell of glassware, watchmakers and radical politics, the London of pristine and uniform-red double-deckers, of Red Bus Rovers that allowed me to ride across and right around Greater London proud to be a Londoner – Civis Londinius Sum – living in a city that had yet to flog off its family silver to the highest bidder. A London pre-privatisation, pre-deregulation, pre-Thatcher, pre-PFI, pre-PPP and pre- every other demeaning, degrading, insulting, petty, penny-pinching policy devised by cynical politicians to keep London down.

The London we dream of, individually or collectively, is either a London we've lost – the City of my early childhood with its working wharves, the London of cockney markets and Covent Garden when toffs still picked their way through vegetable-strewn streets to the

Royal Opera House, of King's Road when it actually swung – or a London that we'd like to create, yet can't agree on or don't know how to achieve. The much-vaunted flexibility and freedom of the city, its apparent resistance to long-term planning, makes it hard to see how anything can get done and how a better London could be planned. Does it need to be planned? What is a better London, and better for whom? These are some of the other questions that drive this book.

Things do get done in London, but often at the last moment, in a hurry and usually only when the money is on the table. Consider, for instance, the recent explosion in coffee bars. Coffee drinking is the big new thing and suddenly London has more coffee bars than you'd think the city could support. Loft living is in. Swoosh. Estate agents have set up in Clerkenwell, Shoreditch and Borough offering the latest in luxury, urban living. Say farewell to commuting misery, hello to billboards depicting perfect, airbrushed couples looking lovingly into one another's eyes over a decaff cappuccino or glass of fresh orange juice. Or enjoying yet another pillow fight (a curious, if common, fantasy among estate agents).

In the mid-1980s the big new thing was the deregulation of the financial markets. Brrrmm. In came the Porsches, the broad-shouldered offices of marble-clad Broadgate, the rebuilding of Liverpool Street station and the Wall Street culture that defined Yuppiedom. It fizzled out, in 1989, as quickly as a bottle of champagne without a trader's silver spoon in it. Down with it came ambitious plans drawn up by Norman Foster to rebuild King's Cross, a concatenation of towers around an impressive new public park. Down went the plan to build Crossrail, a main-line railway link between Paddington and the City. Down went property prices that had reached vertiginous heights in the late 1980s and made many people fear, perhaps for the first time, that they would never be able to get their foot on the first rung of the slippery London property ladder.

The experience of 1980s' London seemed so South Sea Bubble-ish, so very precarious, that the smart talk finally turned to planning. London's shortcomings were compared to the shining example of Paris. It's not that Paris was, or is, in any way perfect, but rather that it did seem to know how to run a transport system well, how to invest in memorable new public architecture, how to keep small businesses in its centre-most streets and how to ensure that people still lived at reasonable rents in even the most chic arrondissements.

Nothing, though, could make London plan. Or so it seemed. In fact, it did the opposite. In 1986, at the height of her powers, Mrs Thatcher abolished London's elected government, the Greater London Council. Now the boroughs were free from "Red Ken" Livingstone and all his socialist tricks. Now council houses could be sold with abandon and the public infrastructure divided up, flogged off and debased. London Transport was broken into pieces, its magnificent workshops and depots, once visited by crocodiles of schoolchildren, sold off to become business parks or shopping malls. Or turned into museums. Air rights were traded over once-proud railway stations, so that exhausted commuter trains and their human cargo were delivered to platforms dark under the superstructure of overbearing post-Modern offices, like those at Charing Cross and Liverpool Street. British Rail architects (long disbanded) fought a heroic and partly successful rearguard action to stop the whole of Liverpool Street station being buried beneath a tombstone of offices.

Everything was for sale. Very Arthur Daley. Very London.

Today it's New Labour politicians who carry the torch for free-market economics. They appear to have no love of London, seeing it only as some sort of cash cow that can be worked twenty-four hours a day. Of course, they pay lip-service to the capital, but the cliches have become numbing. London: Global city. Cultural melting pot. Cosmopolitan. Hub of creative industries. More artists per square inch than any other city in the world. Blah, blah, Blair.

What these politicians find hard to say, because they've failed to deliver it, is that London needs patient investment and long-term planning to ensure its future success and that, being a sentimental city beneath its cocksure exterior, its residents might choose, even if they don't need to, to spare some change for its poor and its down-and-outs and even some thought for its key workers. It needs government to be less meddlesome in the workings of the city's elected authority, and it needs a few more grand public projects, like the Jubilee Line extension, to prove to people that a bigger, better spirit exists than that which has been obvious over the past twenty or so shop-crazy years. The day-to-day structure of the city needs welding together by something more solid than private capital and big business. And, precisely because London is, at heart, a city of shopkeepers and wide-boys, it needs someone, some body, to show it how to be big-hearted, public-spirited and much more civic-minded.

A couple of days before I wrote this, I went to eat with friends in Middlesex Street ("Petticoat Lane" on Sundays). I stopped to take in a scene that seemed, for that moment anyway, to sum up London's gloriously mongrel character. I was standing on the corner of Wentworth Street. The recently painted shop sign before me was in Russian. To my left, a Jewish ladies' knickers shop that's been there for ages. In front, a Bengali restaurant and a Rolls-Royce Silver Shadow with import-export number plates. An Irish couple walked by exploring the limitations of Anglo-Saxon expletives. And all around, the skeletons of blue-steel market stalls waiting for the piles of Gucci and Versace rip-offs, the bangles and baubles that will bring the street flash-harrying into life on Sunday morning. Behind this, a gleaming white luxury apartment block for young professionals, and looming above the lot like a bully in a school playground the bulky frame of Broadgate which made me think of Ronnie and Reggie Kray dressed in Saville Row pin-stripes, running The Firm, doing a bit of business. For better or worse, this is London. Where the Krays got it wrong – shootings, stabbings, torture and general villainy aside – was that, like so many London businessmen and the politicians who suck up to them, they had learned to milk their city rather than to nurture it, as Frank Pick, my London hero who you can read about on the following pages, did.

CIRCUS No. 1

Now, what did the Dome cost? Let's get this right, as far as anyone can. The structure itself, that immense lightweight Dan Dare pairing of Ralph Tubbs's Dome of Discovery and Powell and Moya's Skylon (those twin revolutionary designs from the 1951 Festival of Britain), cost £45 million. What the other £723 million (and the rest) went on was what went inside the Richard Rogers' designed Dome. And this was a waste of energy as well as money. With luck, a truly popular new use will be found for the Dome – a giant greenhouse, a huge food market, maybe – and it will no

longer lie stranded on the banks of the North Greenwich peninsula like some washed-up jellyfish. The big problem with the Dome is the sour taste it has left in people's mouths. The political hype that surrounded the Millennium Experience was at the very least embarrassing. To criticise the project was, in the eyes of New Labour politicians, tantamount to sedition. Championed by Peter Mandelson, the sinister Minister-without-Portfolio, it promised visitors the most fantastic day out in their lives. Well, not quite so fantastic as walking the dog in Greenwich Park, or going to get some chips. Not very fantastic at all really. The Millennium Experience, its entrance flanked by a branch of McDonalds, proved to be an exhibition of corporate sponsorship. The future the Dome was meant to represent appeared to be something to do with burgers, out-of-order rides and commercial propaganda. The next-door neighbour's cat could have told us that for the price of a tin of Whiskas.

HOLD
ON
VERY
TIGHTLY

F rank Pick. A name of two blunt syllables that define the honest and principled man who is one of London's great unsung heroes, and whose uncommon mix of vision and common sense we could do with today. Urgently.

Frank Pick was a sandy-haired Fenman born into a devout Congregationalist family in Spalding, Lincolnshire in 1878. He trained as a lawyer at London University, then worked as a solicitor with the North Eastern Railway at York before settling in London in

1906. Here he began his long association with the complex group of companies that was to become the London Passenger Transport Board (LPTB), a public corporation charged with co-ordinating and running the capital's public-transport network. Although a shy and reserved man, Pick was appointed chief executive in 1933, under the chairman-ship of the politically astute and socially adept Lord Ashfield (Albert Stanley). Theirs was a dynamic and hugely successful part-nership. Within their first five years of office, they had not only fully integrated the capital's bus, tram and Underground services, but had given physical shape to an organisation that was universally consid-ered the finest of its type in the world.

Nothing, thought Pick, was too good for London. Whether it involved the design of buses, trolleybuses, trams and trains, stations, bus shelters, staff canteens and posters, only the best would do. In 1916, for instance, he commissioned a new alphabet from Edward Johnston, the distinguished calligrapher, for use throughout London's transport network. The result was a superb, modern sans-serif interpretation of the lettering that adorns Trajan's column in Rome (as well as the cover of this book) and which has been used ever since on London buses, Tube trains, stations, timetables, display blinds and posters. Here, in a pre-bread and circuses era, was a harking back to a more noble aspect of ancient Rome which Pick decided was well deserved by modern London.

Pick worked long, intense days from the LPTB headquarters at 55 Broadway over St James's Park Underground station. His one-time

publicity officer, the editor and architect Christian Barman, described a typical Pick meeting to inspect the system: Rendezvous, Victoria station 2215hrs, travelling to Holland Park and Aldgate East. Adjourn, 0300hrs. Pick oversaw and planned every last detail of his public transport empire. He travelled it frequently, taking copious notes in his unexpectedly flamboyant green handwriting, ensuring that no fire bucket was left unfilled, no escalator out of service for longer

One of Charles Holden's Piccadilly Line stations

than absolutely necessary. He walked each bus route. He gave a palette of talented young artists, architects, engineers and designers their first break: Charles Holden was awarded the London Architecture Medal in 1929 for his superb new Piccadilly Line stations, his ambition having been, he said, to create "an architecture as pure and true as a Bach fugue". (Holden also designed the fluted bronze uplighters that lined the steps and sides of warm-wood escalators and lit them with a soft glow right up until the Kings Cross fire in 1987.) Seat fabrics for buses and Tube trains were designed by such talents as Enid Marx, Marion Dorn and the painter Paul Nash. It was as if Pick were planting and tending a beautiful garden. The LPTB's "undertaking", he told his fellow directors and departmental officers in 1938, "is a declaration of faith by the Board that its task is worthwhile, that its labours shall eventually contribute their appointed share to the transformation of urban civilisation into some fine flower of accomplishment."

Pick resigned on a matter of principle in 1940 and was appointed Director of the Ministry of Information, Britain's propaganda arm housed in Charles Holden's Senate House. Characteristically, Pick, whose war effort had so far included the successful emergency evacuation of thousands of children from central London, refused to sanction propaganda directed at the enemy that failed to tell the literal truth. He was interviewed by the prime minister Winston Churchill at 10 Downing Street. Pick had already turned down both a knighthood and a peerage. "Mr Pick," Harold Nicolson recalled Churchill saying, "Dover was heavily shelled from the French coast yesterday. I shall be at Dover myself tomorrow, and it is quite possible that I myself may be killed by one of those shells. If that should happen to me, it would give me great comfort to know that a few hours before my death I had spoken to a man who had never told a lie." When Pick left the room, Churchill, well aware of his extraordinary talents, turned to the company and asked, in the spirit of Henry II to his knights when plotting to free himself of the quarrelsome Archbishop of Canterbury and future saint Thomas à Becket, "Who will rid me of this impeccable busman?"

Pick died the following year, having written *Paths to Peace*, an inspiring cross between a planning manifesto and a latter-day *Pilgrim's Progress*. He went to the grave plain Mr Frank Pick. Shortly after his death a last essay of his was published in the *Congregational Quarterly*. Pick was recalling a holiday walking through the Swiss Alps: "All at once, at about 10,000ft above sea level there seemed to come an extraordinary shift of colour. The blue band of the sky had come down to earth and was enveloping the land. Nature works by leaps at critical points and it seemed to me as though Heaven had come down to earth. Above the sky had almost a hard whiteness. The whiteness of God. We were coming face to face."

Lesser and more earthly contemporaries found Pick rather frightening, even dictatorial. Those he respected found him immensely generous and kind. Pick was one of those people of whom it would be said "He did not suffer fools gladly". He didn't; but he was the practical and visionary driving force behind the infrastructure and management of an extraordinarily successful urban public-transport system. The architectural historian Nikolaus Pevsner described him as the Lorenzo the Magnificent of the twentieth century, and the LPTB as a "civilising agent". Of Pick, Kenneth Clark, then Director of the National Gallery (and later "Lord Clark of Civilisation") said, "In a different age, he might have become a sort of Thomas Aquinas."

London Transport, Renaissance Florence and medieval scholastic philosophy in one and the same breath. It seems hard to believe now. Hard too to believe that it was London Transport to whom Joseph

Stalin and his commissars turned for advice when they decided to build the Moscow Metro in 1932. Stalin was grateful for Pick's contribution and awarded him an Honorary Badge of Merit medal (which I was surprised to find when I catalogued Pick's private papers with Bernard Johnson some years ago). Given Pick's involvement, it seems logical enough that the Moscow Metro remains a magnificent achievement, with its heroic stations and spotless trains that serve them every sixty seconds or so for most of the day. What is less logical is that, while both London and Moscow have become ultra-capitalist, retail- and club-crazy cities over the past decade, Moscow maintains a superb, publicly owned Metro plugged into a fully integrated public-transport network, while London treats its public-transport system – if it can be called a system – with what appears to be utter contempt.

The LPTB was created, following an act of parliament devised and promoted by Herbert Morrison, in 1933. This was a time, rather like now, when transport provision in London was in the hands of a number of disparate and competing companies: five railway companies, fourteen municipal tramways, three company-owned tramways, sixty-six bus and coach companies and sixty-nine other companies provided road passenger transport in the city. It made sense at the time to impose a high, uniform standard of public transport throughout the capital. London's population was heading for its 1939 peak of 8.6 million, the impact of private car usage was beginning to be felt and there was a feeling at large that London should set the pace for a high standard of public provision in health, education, transport, civic leadership and responsibility.

Funding was of course always an issue, but it was resolved with no great heartache by the LPTB. The "crucial feature", as Michael Young, who had worked with Morrison, wrote (*Guardian*, 23rd of July 2001), was that the new LPTB "was able to raise its own money by issuing its own various bonds. … About the bonds, Morrison said in [parliamentary] committee that 'stockholders will have no more control over the policy or programmes of the board than the holders, for instance War Loan or Funding Loan, have over the conduct of the national economy." In other words, Pick and Ashfield were able to run a public corporation raising funds where they saw fit, with little day-to-day interference from government and none from the private sector. They worked exclusively in the public interest but without their hands tied by political or economic dogma. And they were hugely successful.

If Pick and Ashfield's LPTB was in any way flawed, it was in the fact that they were charged with making a profit and paying dividends. This was possible in the days when public transport was king and the private car had just entered its long adolescence. But, to ensure their financial success, Pick and Ashfield extended the Underground wherever it seemed likely that new housing and thus new season-ticket holders would follow in its wake. Pick was well aware of this politically determined folly: to meet financial targets, the Underground needed more passengers. More passengers could be generated by extending existing lines and creating a new, outer suburbia where previously there had been market gardens, old Middlesex villages and forgotten parish churches faced by hayfields ploughed by horses. In fact, this spread of the London Transport network, which included the Green Line coach and Green Country bus routes that took the famous LT logo deep into rural Hertfordshire, Essex, Kent, Surrey, Middlesex, Buckinghamshire and Berkshire, caused Pick much concern. Was London getting literally beyond itself?

A fleet of RTL and RT buses at Stockwell Garage, 1953 (over)

Perhaps. But Pick believed, as his five-year plan for London Transport New Works Programme 1935-40 proves – a plan interrupted by Britain's declaration of war with Germany on the 3rd of September 1939 – that the Underground network could be sensibly extended to interchange points on what is now the M25, London's outer wall.

Whatever the problems inherent in such an extensive urban transport network, Pick's over-riding belief that standards of public-transport provision should be uniform throughout the capital remains as valid as it is ennobling. Whether you hailed from Stepney or South Kensington, Arnos Grove or Amersham, Pick believed you should be treated equally and well. So superb, custom-designed and engineered buses and trains met Londoners and took them about their business and off to play. Those who operated them were well paid by the standards of the day. They wore smart uniforms. They were respected for the jobs they did. If not the heart, London Transport represented the free-flowing veins and arteries of the capital.

As a child I knew these trains, buses and stations were special. I liked the fact that RT, RF and RM buses were painted the colours of guardsmens' uniforms – scarlet, gold, black and white – and that they were designed as a form of mobile architecture, to enhance the streets they served. I went, like so many London schoolchildren, to see how the buses were completely rebuilt every few years at Aldenham Bus Depot near Elstree film studios. Aldenham was where Cliff Richard and his chums, fictional London Transport bus workers, set off on Summer Holiday (with Una Stubbs and Susan Hampshire in tow) aboard an RTL – not a Routemaster – double-decker in 1962. We watched RT and Routemaster buses in action on the skid-pad at the Chiswick Bus Works. I later drove them there myself. We saw Tube trains being serviced at Acton Works. We went to Open Days at Neasden depot. We were justly proud and rightly in awe of such a munificent and consistently well-designed transport system. And, of course, it ran like clockwork. This isn't a myth. Few were the days until fairly recently when the Tube could be blamed for lateness at school or the office.

In 1948, along with the main-line railways, London Transport was nationalised. Although prey to subsequent "stop-go" economic policies by successive governments, it was able to hold its own until the rising problem of private-car ownership and traffic congestion in the 1950s. Incomes and consumer spending were finally rising after nine years of austerity. Ration books were phased out in the summer of 1954 and the economy finally began to boom, as Harold MacMillan proclaimed in his famous electoral slogan "You've never had it so good." Good meant traffic jams, pollution and buses being held up. Good meant rising expectations leading to increasing industrial unrest. London's bus drivers went on all-out strike in 1958, a situation that encouraged more people than ever to buy cars and motorbikes.

If London Transport was able to soldier on pretty well during these years it was because of the intelligent investment made in the network by Pick and Ashfield in the 1930s. By the early 1960s, though, major new investment and planning was essential. The Wilson governments of 1964–70 helped with the financing of the ultra-modern Victoria Line opened in 1968, but also helped to undermine London Transport with Barbara Castle's 1968 Transport Act. This effectively prevented LT from designing and building its own buses; from now on grants for new buses, which had become necessary, would be given only for the purchase of new vehicles that followed Department of Transport regulations. In future, new city buses would have to feature doors for safety reasons. No more hopping on and off buses along Oxford Street or elsewhere along slow rush-hour roads. LT was forced to give in, which is why no new

Routemaster buses were built after 1968. This legislation, a nonsense for Londoners, is now enshrined in EC law. (Though a quiet, behind-the-scenes battle is in progress to amend it so that a new generation of Routemasters can take to the road in coming years. The Vehicle Design department of the Royal College of Art is gearing itself up to the challenge.)

In 1970, control of London Transport was handed over to the GLC. By this time, LT services beyond the GLC boundary had been transferred to local authorities or to the National Bus Company. Within a couple of years, philistines in these organisations had undone Pick's work: a wilfully provincial look, service and fleet of vehicles replaced London Transport's urbane style and civilising influence. In central London, meanwhile, the GLC used London Transport as a showcase for political ideas and social experiments. Ken Livingstone's famous "Fares Fair" policy saw an upsurge in bus usage which had been falling since the mid-1950s.

Public-transport systems never run well when used as political shuttlecocks, however, and London Transport was no exception. In 1984, two years before the GLC was abolished, Mrs Thatcher's government took London Transport back under state control. This to-ing and fro-ing could only hinder and delay investment plans and discourage both existing management and anyone seriously interested in working in urban transport. London's buses were now hived off to private companies. (Mrs Thatcher had been much taken with the policies of her pal, the murderous Chilean dictator General Pinochet, to deregulate bus services in Santiago.) The new London privateers, back in jolly-roger action from the mid-1980s, painted their buses any colour under the sun. Each tried to out-do its rivals in choosing the most lurid and childish liveries for buses which they now bought with churlish abandon from any old manufacturer and coachbuilder. The Tories were delighted. The power not only of the former GLC, but of London itself, always a threat to insecure governments, could be seen to be ebbing away. One of the key symbols of London, the custom-designed, standardised red London double-decker, was being replaced with provincial junk. In Tory eyes, red was not only the colour of London, but also that of socialism. (Since then, most of central London's buses have been painted red again, although not in the spirit of socialism. But they are wilfully ugly, claustrophobic, noisy – all those hisses, roars and screeches new to London streets – and a continuing and knowing put-down of London Transport's once proud design and engineering legacy.)

The Greater London Authority (GLA), established in 2000, set up Transport for London (TfL), an organisation headed by Bob Kiley to which London Transport reports. Kiley believes that the real rot set in the 1980s. "Over that period," he says, "marked by government indifference reflected in managerial mistakes and erratic and inadequate funding, the myth has developed that public employees are incapable of managing and running the Underground, justifying the decision to hand it over to the private sector" (quoted in the *Guardian*, 23rd of July 2001). This might well be true, but the real problem is the break-up of London Transport into a large number of private bus companies and a demoralised Underground; this, and the threat of the absurd public-private partnership (PPP) programme devised by the Blair government which threatens the Underground with years of uncertainty.

The debate over the future financing of the London Underground is both frustrating and wasteful. What Londoners really want to know is why, while virtually every other city in the world invested in integrated public-transport systems, London was dragged, and continues to be dragged, in the opposite direction. Why even the possibility of its being split in terms of finance, management, structure or any other way is mooted. And why any of it should be allowed to fall into the hands of business people who have an eye more for the profit to be made on property development above stations – more bread, more circuses – than they have on tracks, trains and signals.

Public transport is one area where London needs rigorous, heavy-duty, civic-minded and almost draconian planning to get itself back into shape. It needs to invest in a new publicly owned and publicly accountable body, much like the old London Transport, to oversee and run a revitalised system. Finance could be raised through bonds as it was when Bob Kiley pulled the ailing Boston and New York subways around in the 1990s: as Kiley has suggested, this would be done through a combination of government financing (London subsidises the rest of Britain, and the whole country would benefit from a more efficient capital), local corporate taxation (all companies benefit from transport that runs on time), and charges made against private transport in favour of public transport. The last of these is partly attended to by the GLA's recently announced £5 charge for entry into the centre of London – not that that will bother many of the city's more wealthy citizens – but the others require concerted action by a far wider range of bodies.

A newly energised London Transport would need to set about restoring the ethos of public service and establishing a system which integrates all transport services – buses, Tubes, mainline trains, river buses, trams, etc. All of these services need improvement of some form or another, but the Underground is probably crying out for it most. The tales of broken-down escalators, long gaps between trains and claustrophobic hold-ups in tunnels are legion, but what about the bare facts? They illustrate both the scale of the challenge and the lack of creativity in rising to it. Three million passengers are carried every day on London Underground (compared with 4.4 million in Paris and 4.7 million in New York – I use these two cities as being similar in terms of wealth); the cost of a ticket here ranges from 90 pence to £5.30 (flat fares of 80 pence and £1.03 in Paris and New York respectively); London's tracks stretch to 253 miles, with 12 lines and 275 stations (131 miles, 14 lines and 297 stations in Paris; 656 miles, 25 lines and 468 stations in New York). The big difference, unsurprisingly, lies in funding: the French RATP's current

annual budget is £780 million, sourced exclusively from state and local bodies (taxpayers, in other words); New York's system, which also covers the bus network, is funded through earnings from fares and other operating revenues (£1.6 billion in 2000) and bond proceeds and government funding (£1.3 billion). London Underground's government grant for 2001-02, by contrast, was just £520 million, with all additional funding being sourced from ticket sales, property rentals, vending machines, payphones and advertising. The government estimates that around £13 billion over 15 years would be made available through the PPP scheme: this is intended to be used for renewing and upgrading the Underground's infrastructure (tracks and trains) which would then be owned by private corporations; responsibility for train operations, signalling and safety would remain in the public sector. Whether there'll ever be any money for other things London Underground desperately needs – like the long-delayed Tube line first mooted by Frank Pick's team in the 1930s, which would link Wimbledon via Putney and the King's Road, with a stop at Chelsea Town Hall, to Walthamstow and Hackney via Dalston – remains to be seen.

There are pressing needs in other areas of London's transport system too – major new railway lines like the much-delayed Crossrail linking Paddington and the City at Liverpool Street via the West End. It should, eventually, get the long-promised Eurostar link via North Kent and Stratford to St Pancras, and it might, with Peter Hendy of the GLA in charge, get more useful traffic on to the Thames, London's majestic natural thoroughfare which is currently woefully underused.

Hendy, a former number 11 bus driver incidentally, is the driving force behind the exemplary new Croydon tram network. Immediately popular and successful, the Croydon Tramlink connects Croydon's intensely busy shopping centre and stations with Wimbledon, Beckenham and the housing estates of New Addington. The sleek, safe and quiet trams (built in Austria because it's virtually impossible to get heavy-duty machinery built in Britain any more) have scotched the idea that trams are old-fashioned or in any way unappealing, and plans are afoot to replace several of London's bus routes – the 68 from Croydon to Chalk Farm (over Waterloo Bridge and under Kingsway where the old, double-deck tram tunnel still remains) and the 207 from Shepherd's Bush to Uxbridge along the Uxbridge Road – with a new generation of

Croydon's Tramlink

modern and reliable machines. Trams are an inherently urban form of transport, and once the initial (admittedly heavy) investment is made in tracks, overhead electric catenary and the trams themselves, a city's transport authority will want to run them for all they're worth, with the end result that the service will be regular and reliable, and that more people will be encouraged to leave their cars at home.

Cars are, after all, often cited as one of the biggest problems confronting a successful public-transport system in London. A seemingly unstoppable growth in the use of the private car has been simultaneous with a decline in public-transport finances and an increase in traffic jams, road casualties and pollution. Dual carriageways, ring roads and urban motorways followed in their wake and, when those arteries clogged up, methods to regulate the flow of transport: traffic lights, zebra crossings and Belisha beacons. Parking meters. Traffic wardens. Multi-storey and underground car parks (Park Lane boasted the world's largest with spaces for a thousand cars in 1962). One-way systems. Yellow lines. Red lines. Residents-only parking bays. Parking tickets. Denver clamps. Tow-aways. Speed cameras. Speed humps ("sleeping policemen"). Width barriers. No left turns. No right turns. No U turns (except politicians on business). Emission controls. CCTV. Five-pound admission charge to central London. Perhaps Frank Pick's plan for an extension of the Underground to the outer ring of London made sense after all. Imagine if motorists and their passengers could pull off the M25 into landscaped or underground car parks and ride direct to any part of London by Tube. If these interchanges included essential shops and other services that commuters could use either to or from work – supermarkets, for instance, which should really only be allowed to be built around transport connections – the total number of car journeys made over a week might be reduced substantially.

Frank Pick's view of transport in London was a holistic one. Without doubt he responded to the needs of bus and train passengers, but he was aware too of those of the pedestrian. My own early travels across Greater London were accompanied by an A-Z as well as bus maps. I coloured in the streets I had travelled: blue for those I'd walked, red for those I'd ridden by bus. I don't think I ever expected to fill in the entire gazetteer, but I made a convincing stab at it. This pursuit meant I got to see the elevated concrete streets of Thamesmead as well as Tottenham Court Road, the side streets of Dagenham and Dollis Hill, of Pinner and Peckham. It took me to see the Piranesian stair that spiralled down into the howling nightmare of the Blackwall Tunnell, to the gated lanes of Rickmansworth where I was questioned by the police. They thought I'd come to do a bit of robbing, but I'd only nipped off school to ride the 336B, "Harry's Bus". A 26-seater green GS with the head of a brightly painted Red Indian on its radiator grille, it was the last of its type and empty most of the day.

Later I cycled and, more recently, motorcycled across even more of London and then got to drive, too. I had long given up colouring in the streets of my A-Z, but I had accepted that a Londoner will get around his city by any means, not just the approved bus, Tube and train, but also car, cycle, scooter, motor-scooter, motorbike, taxi, mini-cab, stretch limo, white van, roller skates, skateboard, boat, horse, horse-and-carriage, Shanks's pony … Each has its place, which is why a transport policy for London must be all-embracing.

So London also needs small transport plans – more cycle lanes, more skating routes through parks, and more thought to the way people walk through the city. The answer here is not wholesale pedestrianisation, which not only somehow brings out the worst in British urban design and behaviour (all those grim concrete planters, those ugly benches and tweedy brick paving, blobs of masticated chewing gum, burger cartons and soft-drink cans), but also robs streets of life and makes them seem dead and frightening places at night. Rather, the solution, I can't help feeling, is to allow traffic – part of the lifeblood of a city, after all – to flow wherever sane or possible, without those bone-jarring humps, and to cut new pedestrian paths and alleys through the line of existing streets and, by law, through all new developments. The owners of some of those acres of privatised land in the middle of London might also be encouraged to open up some of their secret gardens, squares and courtyards (in much the same way that "get orf my land" farmers were persuaded to provide ramblers' rights of way). This would enable pedestrians to zig-zag speedily through central London in a succession of Venetian-style passageways. If the routes were busy, they wouldn't be dangerous. And, in the true spirit of the city, Londoners could duck, dive and weave through the centre of town rather than having to negotiate vast roundabouts or walk for what seems like miles out of the way to get around some flashy new office development.

One zig-zag walk I often do is from the City to the flower market at Columbia Road. The A-Z shows this as an area scythed through by some pretty fearsome streets, but my route crosses hardly any main roads. Instead it takes me along raised City walkways, through a park, a Peabody estate, a dissenters' graveyard (Bunhill Fields where William and Catherine Blake are buried), old alleys, a raised garden with a bandstand at its centre, a patch of public garden and into Columbia Road in about twenty-five minutes.

In 1998, Michael Cassidy, a solicitor and former chairman of the City's Policy and Resources Committee, gave a paper to the Corporation of London on the life and working methods of Charles

Tyson Yerkes (1837–1905). Yerkes was the US entrepreneur who spurred on the development of the Chicago and New York subways and who then came to London. Significantly, perhaps, he died, broke, the year before Pick came down to London from York. Cassidy, a member of one of the PPP consortia currently bidding to take over the running of dismembered parts of the Underground, showed that Yerkes had effectively used early PPP methods to electrify what are now the District, Circle and Metropolitan lines (as far as Harrow-on-the-Hill at the time) and to build several new Tube lines.

While it is true that Yerkes was successful in getting things done, he was also pretty crooked, a far cry from the principled public servant that Frank Pick personified. Both Yerkes and Pick were energetic and successful men, but where I imagine Pick the fair and strategically minded captain of one of Nelson's ships, I see Yerkes as a booty-grabbing buccaneer. Today, the latter image is considered far more appealing than the former. Public service be damned and God stand up for pirates. Of course he'll have to, stand up that is: while the arguments rage over how to finance and run it, the Tube is filled daily to overflowing. Move right along the car, please, hold on very tightly, and mind the gap between government policy and common sense.

CIRCUS No. 2

Canary Wharf station, designed by Foster and Partners, is the architectural highpoint of the magnificent extension of London Underground's Jubilee Line (JLE), opened in 1999 in time for the Millennium celebrations held at the Dome further down the line at North Greenwich. The sheer bravura, technical excellence and generosity of the station, a popular tourist attraction, suggest a huge vote of confidence in public-sector design. And yet, for all its cathedral-like qualities, it represents perhaps the last leap of faith into the realm of true public design in a pre-PFI, pre-PPP era.

The fact that this enduring project had to be ready in time for the opening of the year-long Millennium Experience hastened its completion: some of its operating systems, notably the hi-tech signalling employed, were still untried and -tested by the time the first trains thrummed their way from Stanmore to Stratford via Westminster and Canary Wharf. The structural engineering and architectural achievement, however — the JLE was the biggest civic engineering project in Europe at the time of its construction — remain undimmed by this shortcoming. The generosity of its visionary architecture and public spaces was insisted upon by the line's forward-looking chief architect, Roland Paoletti, who had previously been a key member of the team that designed and built the highly successful Hong Kong Metro. If the JLE is a monument to the end of public design in London, it could hardly be more impressive or more moving. And movement - civilised movement, by the people of London for the people of London and their guests - is its *raison d'être*.

MESS
UP THE
MESS

L ondon is not a planned city. This much is common knowledge. There have been plans – that long litany of Wren, Lutyens and the Royal Academy, Abercrombie, Richard Rogers' Urban Task Force – and just before the Luftwaffe did its bit to reshape London in the 1940s, there were no fewer than 133 public bodies nominally charged with planning within the Greater London area. This spelt chaos, of course, but then London has been long used to that. Any parts of the city that have been carefully planned – from Regent's Park, The Mall, Kingsway and Aldwych to Becontree Estate, Thamesmead, Canary Wharf – have always seemed, whether pleasantly or unpleasantly, rather odd.

London, as we've seen, is above all a mercantile city, far too busy being productive, creative and greedy to be planned along the lines of, say, Canberra or Brasilia, or even Paris, St Petersburg, Turin or Vienna – all cities laid out according to rational principles and informed as much by aggrandisement or even altruism as by abstract notions of architecture. Dukes, princes, kings and emperors had little effect on the look and spread of London, and even if we do now have a prince who supports, if somewhat eccentrically, the idea of conservation, Georgian terraces are still being torn down and replaced by brassy post-Modern office blocks, while even Spitalfields, a remarkable Georgian survivor, is pocked with neo-Georgian houses better suited to the fringe of Bracknell or the hem of Basingstoke than the historic and architectural density of London E1.

While a few key planning issues are widely discussed – the height and placing of a new generation of proposed skyscrapers, the future of the North Greenwich peninsula, the development of the Lea Valley, the timing of Heathrow's Terminal 5 – London carries on doing what it's been doing for a century or more: it sprawls. London has always sprawled because the landscape allows it to; it sits in a huge bowl

Canary Wharf

threaded through by the River Thames. And as it has crept gradually, sometimes slowly, sometimes more quickly, up the sides of the bowl it has witnessed in *excelsis* the phenomenon of suburbanisation.

It is hard to exaggerate the scale and pace of the rush to the suburbs. In 1901, the population of inner London was almost identical to that of what we now know as Greater London. The balance changed, dramatically so, in the 1930s, with the suburbs offering an escape into a world of fresh air, safe cycling, tennis clubs, golf courses, bright shopping arcades and the real countryside just behind the woods or over the next hill. The 1901 populations of Hayes and Ruislip-Northwood, for instance, were 2,594 and 3,566 respectively; by 1939, they had risen to 50,040 and 47,760. Between 1918 and 1938, private firms built 618,571 new houses in Greater London; the LCC and boroughs added a further 153,188. During this period, the balance tipped and the population of inner London dropped and continued to drop for many years to come as that of Outer London skyrocketed. Nearly one and a half million Londoners took to the suburbs, dreaming of a "Detached Country Residence" on the Nonsuch Estate at Cheam or a "Bijou Baronial Hall" on the Merrylees Estate, Hendon. "Live in Ruislip where the air's like wine/It's less than half an hour on the Piccadilly Line", went an optimistic rhyming advert by local builders George Ball Ltd. Or why not choose South Norwood, described rather hopefully in a 1936 brochure as "London's smallest Garden city".

The rush to this unplanned, land-gobbling suburbia placed an onus on the railways and bus companies. Between 1930 and 1937, for instance, the annual number of passengers using Rayner's Lane station on the Metropolitan and District/Piccadilly lines rose from 22,000 to 4 million. The LPTB responded by intensifying the exodus, extending lines, adding routes and increasing the level of services, thereby encouraging London to sprawl further than it might have if the railways had refused to play ball with gung-ho housebuilders (although Frank Pick, its chief executive, was later to campaign successfully for London's Green Belt).

Not everyone approved of the idea of suburbia, of course. A 1935 article had this to say of Stoneleigh Park: "These people have been lured here by tempting advertisements about living in the country. By coming here in thousands they have defeated their own object – the country has disappeared – a new suburb has been built and the true gainers are the builders, estate agents and multiple-shop owners." The same article could be written in 2001 of the latest generation of suburbs. And perhaps it will be written again in 2066 when EC-owned maglev (magnetic levitation) trains whizz London commuters to the new suburbs in Wick, Stranraer, Pwllheli and Newquay.

John Betjeman (born in Highgate, 1906, died Chelsea, 1984) published his infamous poem "Come friendly bombs and fall on Slough" in 1937:

Mess up the mess they call a town –
A house for ninety-seven down
And once a week a half-a-crown
For twenty years

Mellowed by 1954, Betjeman was rueful rather than angry about the triumph of suburbia. His poem "Middlesex" begins

Gaily into Ruislip Gardens
Runs the red electric train,
With a thousand Ta's and Pardon's
Daintily alights Elaine

It moves on to recall a rural Middlesex, a place of weekend excursions for Londoners in the poet's childhood and now buried under a rash of red bricks, a forest of Mock-Tudor beams:

Parish of enormous hayfields
Perivale stood all alone,
And from Greenford scent of mayfields
Most enticingly was blown
Over market gardens tidy,
Taverns for the bona fide,
Cockney anglers, cockney shooters,
Murray Poshes, Lupin Pooters*
Long in Kensal Green and Highgate silent under soot and stone

*London characters from George and Weedon Grossmith's satirical *Diary of a Nobody*, 1892; originally a column in *Punch* and still a bestseller.

For all this, London suburbia remains sacrosanct, and all wise critics as well as those with rat-like cunning know well to pay lip service to it. Partly because few observers dare go against the fiercely and morally indignant conservative grain of Middle England, suburbia basks, like a shark, in its capacity to grab as much land as it says it needs to grow in. Now, however, as Greater London threatens to spill over the sides of its natural bowl, even the hard-fought-for Green Belt, established in 1938, is under threat.

There is no one obvious answer as to what London can do to halt its growth, and no consensus either on whether such a halt is desirable or not. But what is known is that new solutions are needed urgently to cope with its growing population (approximately 7.2 million today, and rising at something like 28,000 a year). One possibility is to increase the population density of the inner areas, not the suburbs. This would require a cleaning up and new investment in some of the city's "backwaters"; it would also mean, very importantly, imposing some sort of regulation on land and property prices – by linking them to income in some way.

There are one or two good existing examples of how city-centre living in London can be made attractive, even when homes are surrounded by main roads and offices. The Corporation of London's Barbican housing development (1957–82), for instance, designed by the architects Chamberlin, Powell and Bon, features fine gardens, lakes and fountains, carp, ducks and birdlife (wrens, magpies, wood pigeons, blackbirds). The mountainous concrete structure of the apartment blocks deadens sound and it can be as quiet here as in any

The Barbican housing development

London park or garden square. And, east of the City, the A13 arterial road now passes under a "green bridge", designed by Piers Gough of CZWG architects and planted with grass, trees and flowers. It forms a link between two existing stretches of parkland and reconnects what had been an artificially divided community.

All new housing developments should include in-built facilities like shops, playgrounds and swimming pools, which have traditionally only ever been provided for the very well off. New York and much of continental Europe provide examples of densely occupied apartment blocks that are connected at street level to any number of essential and useful services from coffee shops to laundries, bakeries and hairdressers, that make city-centre living much easier than the look of their streetscapes suggest. Another leaf from the European book might be publicly owned covered markets, along the lines of those that are a feature of each of Paris's arrondissements. These offer spaces at low rents to small traders, a chance to buy and sell fresh produce and other goods. Markets then become a natural part of the street scene, helping to keep an area busy and lively, and giving local residents an important sense of neighbourhood.

Another possibility, something of a middle course between the new-town sprawl and the back-to-the-inner-city option, is to urbanise the suburbs. This, of course, sounds like a contradiction in terms, but the point is this: if suburbs could provide more employment than they do, then the need to commute from them either into or out of town would most probably fall. And the more urbanised they become – with a solid local labour market and convenient facilities – the more likely that businesses wishing to avoid central London's extortionate rental rates will want to relocate to them. Naturally, there will always be people who want to escape the suburbs altogether, as there will be those for whom suburbia is a

Piers Gough's "green bridge" in Hackney

sacred place for rest and relaxation only, but just as Croydon longs to be a city, so there are many London suburbs that could become small towns. Their centres need to be built up, leaving their avenues, groves and cul-de-sacs free for lawn-mowing, Mondeo-washing and the instilment of irreproachable Middle – England values. This would certainly suit politicians of right (New Labour), centre (Lib-Dem) and uncertain (Tory) leanings. The more suburbanised London becomes, the less radical and the more passive its electorate. Recall the more recent, "political" suburbanisation of London when most of the once heavily unionised industries moved out of town or closed down after the 1960s, followed by the newspaper presses, the docks and the power stations in the 1980s. London politics have been a whole lot softer since then.

One of the problems in trying to solve planning issues is the need for a coherent voice: those keen at the moment to get a planning grip on London are already falling into the trap of dividing their kingdom into one that Lear might have shaped, raising the fear that the kingdom will eventually fragment. Planning discussions and architectural matters in London are currently the province of Westminster, in the guise of the Government Office for London; the GLA and its new Architecture and Urbanism Unit chaired by Richard Rogers and run by Ricky Burdett of the London School of Economics; the Department of Culture's Commission on Architecture and the Built Environment (CABE), chaired by the property developer Stuart Lipton; the Department of the Environment; the planning departments of local authorities; and a host of less official lobby and pressure groups.

Yet, as Frank Pick wrote, "even the most expert critics will make ludicrous mistakes and perpetrate extraordinary contradictions with a change of style or fashion". Or, he might have added, patronage. Planning fads and fashions are as much dependent upon who's in and who's out, whose coat-tail is best hung on to, and which is the best way up the treacherous and slippery path of ambition, as it is upon common sense. For Pick as for most of us, the best way forward is education. "The duty of criticism", he wrote, "is a matter for all citizens". But to be a good critic, you need to have studied hard, to have read widely, thought as far as your mind will stretch, travelled extensively and used your imagination to the full. London's education system is all too rarely a match for this ambition. (Some of the city's basic planning issues – how to reduce road traffic, for instance – could be tackled by investment in decent education. If the standard of education across London's schools were more consistent, children would be able to walk to school and the roads would be free of the cars of wealthy parents chauffeuring them to "decent" schools.)

Planning then, like transport, is a holistic subject. It's not just about whether we should build skyscapers or more boring apartment blocks eastwards along the Thames, but about shaping London to fit the needs and the interests of its citizens. But until we learn to convert our aggressively mercantile economy into a true social economy, planning will remain a thing of wishful thinking, tinkering and tampering. The current government obsession with money and business above all else sets a pace that will ultimately be the country's and London's undoing; far too much of the city is currently being planned and redeveloped using crude and dogmatic economic expedients which are forms of mortgaging our futures and holding what remains of the public sector hostage to the cupidities of private interests and the vagaries of the free market.

CIRCUS No. 3

Here's a microcosm, although not that small, of the way London plans in a higgledy-piggledy manner. The rebuilding of the Royal Opera House (ROH) at Covent Garden was a long-drawn-out and, perhaps, appropriately melodramatic affair. But for first-time visitors, the experience of the buildings, with the exception of the plush renovated Victorian auditorium, is anything other than operatic. The new works by Dixon Jones are almost self-effacing, and yet they add up not simply to a much more workable and inviting opera house than before, but to a major rethinking of the

Covent Garden streetscape. Here there are new arcades facing the old market buildings and new ways of walking from Covent Garden piazza to Bow Street. The entire city block which the ROH now occupies is threaded through with a variety of spatial experiences from the rebuilt Floral Hall (once part of the market and now the ROH foyer), to a whizzy ticket hall, roof top cafes under pergolas, a massively reconstructed backstage and decent dressing rooms, a secondary performance space, and, of course, a shop. While all this is no small achievement, it is almost wilfully designed to counteract the bombastic new arts buildings designed under the "grands projets" banner for President Mitterrand in Paris at the time of the bi-centennial of the French Revolution. In comparison with the rather brutal and dominant Bastille Opera, the ROH is a very gentle sequence of buildings knitted together to form a coherent whole.

ANGELS WITH ANGRY FACES

Philip Lawrence's face peered from the front page of the newspapers. That's Philip Lawrence, I thought, without taking in the caption beneath it, as you would when the red-haired man had once been your English teacher. Philip's picture was on the front of the papers because he was dead. Stabbed by a pupil while trying to break up a fight at the gates of the school in Maida Vale where he was the head teacher. It was Philip who had burst into an abbey classroom at a time in my life when I really didn't want to be at school any longer, placed his arms on either side of a desk and launched, intoxicated with words, into

> Beautiful lofty things, O'Leary's noble head,
> My father upon the Abbey stage, before him a raging crowd,
> This land of saints, and as the applause died out,
> Of plaster saints, his beautiful mischievous head thrown back
>
> Standish O'Grady supporting himself between the tables,
> Speaking to a drunken audience high nonsensical words …

And so on to Augusta Gregory seated at her great ormolu table and Maude Gonne awaiting a train at Howth station. All the Olympians, a thing never known again. Philip threw his head back. It was a beautiful, mischievous trick and it worked. The words of Yeats's "Beautiful lofty things" sealed themselves into the choirs of my imagination that day. I may not have smiled at the time, but the love of poetry I half-hid has only grown since.

Philip Lawrence was an inspirational teacher, and a lovely fellow. He became the head at St George's in Maida Vale at a time when so many jobs must have been open to him in the smarter echelons of the private sector. The choice killed him.

As schoolboys, we all knew how to fire a .303 Lee-Enfield (a veteran rifle made in Enfield, dead accurate over a long range), whether members of the toy soldier brigade or not. We even knew how and where to acquire live ammunition. But the thought of killing someone was, I like to think, quite beyond us.

London schools can be tough places, and though, unlike US city schools, guns are virtually unheard of, there are plenty of knives and lots of attitude. London schools can also be models of decorum and scholastic excellence. Standards are as erratic as those of the city's hospitals and buses. A shining crocodile of immaculate doh-ray-me Hill House children, looking like extras from The Sound of Music, children replete with nourishing food and every known vitamin, crosses Knightsbridge on its way to top schools, the best universities, the plummiest jobs and a CBE at the very least. In south London, a near feral pack of kids lurks shiftily around the dramatic new Peckham Library where little Damilola Taylor had been, nine months on from arriving in London from Nigeria, before he was stabbed to death. They ask for smokes and tell me school is rubbish. A waste of space. Which is very possibly, and sadly, how they see themselves, hiding more than a little hopelessly behind unconvincing street-wise facades. Angels with angry faces.

Our education system, or lack of one, can only make anyone who bothers to think about it – most parents, many pupils, all teachers – pretty angry, too. What had been set up in the aftermath of the Second World War as a universal system of high-quality, universally accessible, free education has sunk into yet another of the dim battles being fought between the weakening forces of the undermined public realm and ever-cockier private sector shock troops encouraged and subsidised by government.

Kevin McNeany is chief executive of Nord Anglia, a private

company brought in to run key education services in the meltdown borough of Hackney. He believes that teachers "need the private sector approach, which mixes enthusiasm and a fresh start with strong business practices and an ethos centred on the needs of customers". Strong what? The needs of whom? Where once children played in LCC school sandpits, passengers strap-hung their way to work on the Underground, and customers bought breasts of New Zealand lamb in the marble halls of high-street Sainsbury's, now everyone is a customer consuming London as if it were one giant, drive-thru burger joint.

Michael Murphy is the new head teacher of Crown Woods School in Eltham. Ofsted, British education's regulatory body, says the 2,300-pupil comprehensive is failing. Murphy, who has already "turned around" one failing school, has been brought in to try his magic on Crown Woods. He outlined his programme in a thoughtful article in the *Evening Standard* (25th of July 2001): 44 staff out of 112 to go, 5 deputy heads to manage specific areas of school life including the performance of teachers, school hours to be changed to 8 am to 2.30 pm with just the one 40-minute break for lunch. "Things get a bit flaky towards the end of the day in any school," Mr Murphy told the *Standard*. "Teachers get tired and children get tired. If you front-load the day, you have more focus and pace." And, who, pupil or teacher, thinking back to Double Maths on a hot, summer's afternoon, will disagree? These strategies may or may not work, but surely Michael Murphy is speaking the same business-school language of Kevin McNeany at Nord Anglia? Murphy disagrees; he believes that the scope for the private sector in raising standards in state schools is "minimal". Forcing it on schools, he says, will only further damage morale, deterring would-be teachers at a time when London needs teachers as much as it does bus-drivers and nurses.

"There are some very good managers in [state] schools. There are some very poor managers in the private sector. The government is wrong to think that change can only come from the outside."

Yet what can anyone do with a government – a parliament, too, sadly – so in thrall to big business? Jack Straw, the cabinet minister and head of the National Union of Students in the radical Sixties (not the fourteenth-century radical who lost his head soon after the Peasants' Revolt), sat on the board of governors of Pimlico School when it was agreed recently to rebuild the Seventies' spaceship of a building. The method chosen – private finance initiative (PFI) – was proof that politicians find the real world a foreign land. The governors agreed to throwing in their lot with developers who would build a new school on a tight budget as long as they could have a slice of playground on which to build – guess what? – a block of free-market luxury flats. Not only is the design of the new school decidedly average, but to flog off part of a playground in central London is an act that beggars belief. As to mortgaging the school's finances to satisfy a shabby government dogma, what can anyone say? Irresponsible is the most ingratiating word that comes to mind.

It was the Education Act of 1944 that set Britain's sights on a high standard of free education for all children. Between 1950 and 1970, somewhere across the country, a new school was finished every day. Education mattered. It fell victim, however, to increasingly polarised views on how it should be organised from the 1960s onwards. Today, education policy is run by a mind-numbing arrangement of alliances between local education authorities (LEAs) and the Department of Education (DfEE), and driven through by any number of acronymic and maybe even acrimonious bodies like OFSTED, SENJIT and AMP.

London has suffered particularly since the closure of the Inner London Education Authority by the Thatcher government in 1986. There is now a hotch-potch approach to provision and an increasing disparity between "good" and "bad" schools. Some are becoming so-called specialist schools, offering places to those with a particular talent in, for instance, technology or music, which enables them both to cherry-pick their intake and to bid for money and favours from "interested" sources. Others can't even fund things like repairs to playgrounds and so seek sponsorship from the likes of Nike who then dole out logo-splashed baseball caps and sweatshirts for pupils to wear. Alongside these runs the complex gamut of prep schools, private schools, grammar schools (in the outer boroughs), grant-aided schools, "bog-standard" comprehensives ... While choice might be considered desirable by those who can afford to exercise it,

Kingsdale School, Dulwich

it is the antithesis of the spirit in which the 1944 Act was conceived. (And, come to think of it, shouldn't Nike sooner be investing money in the education of children in south-east Asia, many of whom never get to a school because they're working in sweatshops to produce fashion "goods" for children in the West?)

School Works is one of the brighter clearings in this blackboard jungle. Devised by Hilary Cottam, its energetic director, this charity believes that the current spate of new school buildings, most of them PFI-funded, would fail a basic test in architecture, if there were such a thing. "In Britain, we do spend on schools and other public buildings," says Cottam, "but the architecture is procured insensitively and on the cheap as if the buildings we live and work in have no effect on us physically or psychologically. What we look at is the needs of specific schools. How pupils and teachers feel about them, what they feel they need, how conflicting needs can be resolved and how to make school enjoyable for everyone."

School Works' first major project, in collaboration with the Architecture Foundation and the think tank Demos, is a £9 million overhaul of Kingsdale School, Dulwich, in the borough of Southwark. Separated only by a high wall, Kingsdale stands back to back with the high-achieving Dulwich College. It is a school with a 40 per cent turnover of pupils, many of whom are recent immigrants and "asylum seekers" (as if to say "Red Indians"). But now the pupils as well as the teachers are being empowered. School Works has teamed Kingsdale with imaginative architects de Rijke, Marsh, Morgan to rethink the school's design.

The first task for Steve Morrison, Kingsdale's new head teacher, and his deputy Cathy Bryan, was to ask pupils to make an audit of the school – what worked, what didn't. Their comments, channelled through School Works, made fascinating reading. Pupils said they

Dulwich College

would rather go home than use the school lavatories; but, if they did go home, they probably wouldn't go back to school that day. Girls felt they had no place in the playgrounds because boys took them over to play football. As for public spaces inside the school, they wrote things like "This corridor needs to be trashed." With the help of the architects, they have now made a plan to reshape the school around a new internal public square. Corridors will be abolished, decent lavatories provided and, in general, architectural form will be given to the way teachers, pupils and parents would like to see the school run. It's the first time most of them have even been invited to have a say.

This is one success story among the more common news of declining standards, "sink" schools, ousted heads and excluded pupils. It's an uneven and unfair approach to the education of London's children and it's divisive and harmful, to everyone. So let's stop playing who-can-piss-highest-up-the-wall games − using PFI, PPP and the threat of privatisation as crude weapons to demoralise hard-pressed teachers. Let's stop treating education as if it was some sort of commodity. And let's dedicate a revamped school to the memory of Philip Lawrence to remind politicians, pupils and the rest of us how committed, imaginative and brave London's teachers are and have to be.

CIRCUS No. 4

Five and a half million visitors in its first year. Tate Modern had definitely got something right, especially as the point of this temple of power transformed into cathedral of art was that it should be accessible to as many people as possible. Not just physically, but culturally too. The Tate chose not to design a new building, but to rebuild the redundant Bankside Power Station sited on the Thames immediately to the south of St Paul's Cathedral. This was a far less controversial decision than investing in a new building would have been, and the location is a fine one.

The presence of Tate Modern has undoubtedly boosted the fortunes of this once run-down stretch of Southwark. And yet, for all the accomplishments of its Swiss architects, Herzog and de Meuron, the Tate feels odd. On some days it feels a little too much like Brent Cross or Lakeside — a shopping mall with busy cafes and queues for the lavatories, only with a pretty good art collection. As for the galleries, stacked up on the river side of this Brobdingnagian building, the millions of visitors tend to tramp up and down as if moving along enclosed high streets rather than through a series of calm spaces. There is nowhere for quiet contemplation. Still, if contemporary art is much more of a big street party than it used to be, then perhaps Tate Modern has got everything right. Maybe the blurring that critics and curators like to talk about between advertising, shopping, computer games and art is happening and it's all for the accessible best. Maybe.

BED
D
LAM

Perhaps it was just a normal day for a young London surgeon. Tim Dudderidge was working his 125th hour out of a 130 that week when he cut himself with an instrument that had been used on a seriously ill private patient. The notes at the end of the bed said the patient was HIV positive. "I know I'm a bit of hypochondriac," says Dudderidge over a quick lunchtime pint of orange juice and lemonade in the pub across the road, "but once I'd reported the matter I pumped myself with four different anti-Aids drugs. ... I don't normally cut myself. I think I was getting tired. The good news, for me, was that the reference to HIV was a transcription error. It should have read HCV positive, referring to Hepatitis C. Mind you, until the tests come back, I don't know if I've been infected or not. In any case, Hepatitis A, B or C isn't much fun." Dudderidge sneezes. "I think that's hayfever," he says encouragingly, "or just the start of a cold."

Dudderidge is a senior house officer in the Accident and Emergency (A&E) department at Hampstead's Royal Free Hospital. He qualified as a surgeon in 1998 and worked in Bristol before moving to London. His story of long hours is commonplace among NHS doctors nationwide, as is, alas, his tale of a private patient taking up a bed in an NHS hospital. It is another illustration of the warped way in which public and private have overlapped in the last fifteen or so years.

London's doctors and hospitals are particularly prey to the situation as they are treating the very richest and the very poorest people in the country on a daily basis. But there's also the particularly urban problem – again more marked in London – of a lack of integrated services which should, in theory, mean that people use hospitals only when strictly necessary. As it is, most of the sad waiting rooms of London's overworked A&E departments are half-full of what one medic described as "rubbish patients". She didn't mean to be nasty, but A&E staff are overwhelmed by the sheer number of patients who turn up with complaints so minor that even a GP might feel put upon. Dudderidge recalls a patient who came to A&E recently with a sore throat. "Of course, I checked her out as well as I could; that's our job. But I really couldn't find anything wrong and recommended she gargled with aspirin. It must have done the trick; she didn't come back."

I know what it's like. Some years back, I was one of a number of people knocked over on a zebra crossing on Southampton Row by Mr Angry, a van driver in a red baseball cap. An ambulance was called, but a cabbie kindly took me and a woman and two children, free of charge, round to University College Hospital's A&E. Women and children first, I thought. After a while, though, my leg began to hurt quite a lot and the blood was doing an imitation of the Thames at high tide across the lino floor. I did the Sergeant Wilson of Dad's Army bit, shuffling up to the desk and asking, if she didn't mind awfully, if I could possibly have a brief word with one of the busy doctors on duty. "You'll have to wait your turn like everyone else," she snapped. I'd been marked down as "rubbish" as much as a crop-haired customs officer at Heathrow marks you down as an international drug dealer while the international drug dealers walk past in smart business suits and slimline executive briefcases. But nobody else seemed to be bleeding quite as much as me, and I couldn't see a woman in labour or a boy with his head stuck in a section of railings anywhere. Luckily, a young doctor turned up at the desk and suggested I might possibly like to have my leg looked at. Once on the doctor's side of the desk, everything was fine: a bit of cleaning up, a jab, a neat row of stitches and an X-ray, and a wobble back into the rush hour on Gower Street in bloody trousers. People looked at me as if to say "on the bottle". I don't know if this story is in any way typical, but it does seem to illustrate the crazy way the health system functions here – massive under-resourcing combined with mis- or over-use by a public which feels cheated of its once celebrated national health service.

"The point about the woman with the sore throat", says Dudderidge, "is that she was a single mother, up to her eyeballs with worry and debt, and quite clearly feeling there was absolutely no one she could turn to. So she ends up in A&E. It's not her fault, but it's a sorry situation when someone feels this way."

I have a recurring daydream about health care in London – and why not across the country? – which runs something like this: Why can't schools be equipped with health clinics to serve children and their families? And why can't school gyms become fitness centres for adult or family use at certain times of the week? And libraries be turned over occasionally for general use as a resource centre for the community? That way, schools would become less scary places for adults, and children might feel more connected to an active, "extended family". Further, a more holistic approach to public health might just begin to prevail.

This doesn't get around the matter of hospitals, of course, though it might mean that A&E wards become more sane places. Various "solutions" to our hospital crisis are currently being mooted – shipping patients to other EC countries (Germany, for instance, which despite its much higher population provides twice as many beds per capita than the UK), or even as far afield as India, where medical training is of an exemplary standard – but none of these confronts the very real problem of how most people will be treated once the

One of London's private hospitals

government's PFI hospitals are fully blotted on the landscape or when it becomes more obvious quite how much a US-style system is to be imposed on us.

Recently I went to see my new-born god-daughter, Daisy, in St Thomas's Hospital. It was a bit like going to a run-down steel works in East Germany in the mid-1970s. The lifts were goods lifts. Buttons were missing and they stank. Anybody could walk in. The nurses on duty, hard-pressed as ever, were changing shifts and I was told that Daisy's mother was definitely not there. Not in the hospital. Except she was, because she called out from behind her polyester curtains to attract my attention. What an odd place to come into the world, I couldn't help thinking …

Again, as with schools, there is no London-wide standard. Walk into the Chelsea and Westminster Hospital on Fulham Road and you can hardly believe that this, too, is an NHS hospital. It has Alan Jones and Patrick Heron artworks where other hospitals have Damien Hirst-style installations of patients lying on trolleys in corridors; it has a swish lobby, near-silent escalators and daylight rather than an attack of bright flourescence. There's no good reason why such disparity should exist, unless they have a much smarter kind of accident and illness in Chelsea and Westminster.

Just one change of bus on Fulham Road takes you to St George's Hospital in Tooting. I visited a patient here as a child, my Uncle Sonny, and it frightened me. I used to think of it, despite its mani-cured lawns and rose bushes, as Stalag Luft SW17. No one talked about mental illness then, and they don't much now. More recently I visited a girlfriend's sister at St George's. Nothing much had changed: the smell of bright yellow custard, gray cabbage, pissed-on clothes and sticky biscuits squashed behind seat cushions, the prison-style furniture and décor, the bored guards slouching by each locked door, attendants with a poor command of English, drugs used routinely to keep patients passive because of a shortage of doctors, the simple, often avoidable tragedies of many patients' lives, caused so often by poverty, lack of education and self-esteem, and abuse . . . these things make you fight back tears of frustration. What a waste of humanity. What a way to treat people. Still, at least the crowds don't pay on weekdays to gawk at the mentally ill as they used to at Bedlam in Hogarth's day. They pay to watch actors simulating breakdowns and psychosis on tv and videos instead.

CIRCUS No. 5

Sited on a back street near some of London's great teaching hospitals, the British Museum has fed and nurtured minds, if not bodies, for generations. Lottery funds, on a scale comparable to those given the Tate Modern, were pumped into a major makeover of this great and popular institution and centred around the reconstruction of the Great Court by Foster and Partners. A secret world of what had been storage space crammed into the recesses of the Great Court (previously dominated by the drum-shaped former Reading Room of the British Library) was opened up to the public. Now there

were cafes and shops beating a new rhythm around the old drum housed under a fine new glass roof. But was everybody happy? It seemed as if the mummies of the Egyptian galleries had turned in their sarcophagi, or put a curse on the project. The wrong sort of stone, French instead of English, was used in the construction of a new classical portico leading into the Great Court, and a kind of decidedly unhealthy madness gripped the media, heritage bodies and disgruntled museum trustees as they seized on this as a rod with which to beat the backs of architects who had dared to invade the sanctity of a museum that, after all, thrived on antiquity. The fuss over the stone has since crumbled. The Great Court is undeniably impressive, although with so many sandwiches being eaten here and so much shopping for second-rate souvenirs, it will always be in danger, on busy days, of feeling uncomfortably like an airport departure lounge. A little creative surgery is needed.

PALACES FOR THE PEOPLE

I n the course of researching this book, I went to see Dickon Robinson, chief executive of the Peabody Housing Association, London's largest, in his busy office on Westminster Bridge Road. A genial and astute man, Robinson is one of the few people in what remains of the public sector commissioning, by default, intelligent new low-rent housing in central London. By default? Yes, by default. Without charities like Peabody, there would be nowhere in London for those on low incomes to live. Who else bothers to build new homes in central London for nurses, teachers and bus drivers?

Currently only one in four nurses working in London lives less than a mile from their place of work; 55 per cent live between five and twenty-five miles away. Only one in five bus drivers, one in twenty teachers and one in fifty policemen live less than a mile from their workplace. You can bet that apart from a few hardy cyclists the rest rely on public transport, or, because they work "unsocial" hours, use cars. It's not as if they want to travel so far: of those questioned in a GLA survey in 2000, 64 per cent of bus drivers, 61 per cent of nurses and 49 per cent of teachers said they would like to live closer to their work. Police officers felt a little less strongly, but that may be because they're significantly better paid than drivers and nurses – they were about the only public-service workers to be favoured by Mrs Thatcher and, ironically, have always been well represented by their union, the Police Federation – they are consequently far more likely to own their own homes (67 cent compared with 12 per cent of bus drivers).

Because it's so hard to get a decent and affordable place to live in central London, staff turnover in these jobs is high. Some of the information gathered by the GLA's Affordable Housing Scrutiny Committee in 2000 makes for Alice in Wonderland reading. The privatised bus company Arriva, for example, admitted a staff turnover of 30 per cent a year, with 70 per cent of staff leaving within the first two years to find driving jobs, mostly, in other sectors. Last year, the company spent £115,000 on hotel rooms for drivers hired from Scotland and the north west of England. Housing is nearly always the problem, although low prestige and poor pay – 80 per cent of London bus drivers are paid less than £15,000 a year – must play their part in a driver's decision to quit. Since privatisation, bus drivers' wages have fallen in real terms: evidence from Arriva shows a rise of only £40 a week since 1970, compared with an average increase across all occupations of £165. Where drivers might once have been allocated council homes in the days of the GLC, LCC and Middlesex County Council, most of these have now been sold and even when houses do come on the market they're too expensive for them to buy. The infuriating thing is that at least one solution was often on what was London Transport's doorstep. The company used to own huge tracts of land in the guise of railway works and bus depots and if these had been redeveloped intelligently in a co-ordinated fashion across London, they could easily have incorporated high quality, low-rent housing. Instead, what was Chiswick Bus Works is now Chiswick Business Park.

Average house prices in London are five times the annual income of the average household in the capital. And the monetary issue is compounded by one of demand: the number of single-parent families in London is growing (10 per cent of family households; 14 per cent in Lambeth, the highest in Britain), as are the number of people living alone (50 per cent of households in the City of London; 30 per cent across London generally). Inner London boroughs which from 1939 witnessed the most dramatic exodus of residents to the outer suburbs, the country and the new towns have since 1991 recorded the highest levels of immigration, attracting both the wealthy to prestigious boroughs like Kensington and Chelsea and the City of Westminster, and the poor to cheap, run-down boroughs including Tower Hamlets, Islington, Hackney, Lambeth. These, by the way, are four of the officially poorest ten boroughs in Britain. Thirteen of the country's twenty poorest are in Greater London.

The day before I went to see Dickon Robinson, I was talking to a Spanish visitor who had the impression that Islington was one of the wealthiest parts of London, one of its smartest addresses. After all, didn't Tony Blair live there? Well, he did before he became Prime Minister and moved to Downing Street. I took my visitor for a walk in N1. The Georgian and early Victorian streets set behind Islington's Upper Street, and between here and Canonbury, are indeed quite beautiful. There are lovely canalside walks, cheery pubs, enjoyable antique shops, charming restaurants and some of the smartest people you could ever hope to meet jostling for parking spaces in mountainous four-wheel drive vehicles and battling bravely through the traffic – Spirit of the Blitz and all that – to take little Sebastian to prep school. There is, though, another side to Islington. Turn off Upper Street and walk the length of Essex Road, exploring the streets left and right. I suggested to my visitor that even though he came from Bilbao, a tough city by any standards, he might well find some of these urban backwaters pretty challenging on a Friday night. Rarely does a copy of *Angel*, the local free magazine (named after a famous Islington coaching inn replaced by a post-Modern bank in the early Eighties), drop through my City letterbox without news of a stabbing in one of the estates here. London remains Dickensian in parts. "A bit like your Oliver Twist," suggested my visitor. Sort of, but with satellite tv dishes, wrecked cars, hoods to hide under, and pissed-in lifts.

These places, largely devoid of hope and looked down on, are more medieval than Victorian.

Housing elsewhere in London ranges from the world's most romantic – the stage-set white-stucco neo-Classical terraces built under the direction of John Nash around Regent's Park in the 1820s – to the utterly depressing, like the rows of mean mass-produced Victorian terraces that surround central London in a cheap corset of red-brick, and the gun-law post-war estates like Stockwell Park. Perhaps I shouldn't find this shaming, but I do. I don't think London should be like this, an over-restored Georgian house kitted out with a redundant Aga cheek by jowl with some of the poorest estates in Western Europe.

The Peabody Trust is very much a part of London, and has been ever since the Massachusetts-born philanthropist George Peabody invested £500,000 in a fund "to ameliorate the conditions of the poor and needy of this great metropolis and to promote their comfort and happiness". Starting out in Commercial Street, Spitalfields in 1862, the Trust had housed or rehoused five thousand Londoners in decent, if rather dour new flats by 1890. It was then that the keen young architects of the newly formed LCC began designing more than decent homes for the working class, taking up Peabody's mantle and pioneering the way for inner-city council housing of a quality unknown pretty much before or since in much of Europe. Perhaps it was because the LCC was a new body and eager to prove itself; perhaps it was because its architects were well versed in the socialist and visionary writings of John Ruskin (1819–1900), William Morris (1834–1896), the Social Democratic Foundation, the Fabian Society and Karl Marx (1818–1883). Whatever it was, the LCC Architects'

The LCC's Cleverly Estate in Acton (over)

Department proved itself to be truly inspired when it produced the first of its universally admired estates in Shoreditch. The Boundary Estate, completed in 1898, pivots around Arnold Circus, with its tall trees and battered bandstand. Flats are incorporated into handsome Arts & Crafts blocks, beautifully built and as elegant as any private housing. These were true "people's palaces" and the trick – making beautiful, coherent buildings out of the sophisticated massing of small, family flats – was repeated several times over during the next twenty or so years, culminating in a massive block of flats on the Cleverly Estate, Acton that even looks like Christopher Wren's Fountain Court block for William and Mary at Hampton Court Palace. Such buildings might now be called over the top, but back then the flats were designed as homes for heroes after too many young Londoners had suffered appalling experiences in the Somme and elsewhere during the First World War.

The spirit of Ruskin and Morris was behind more than just housing. It inspired the development of many of London's public baths and lidos – liedoze to Londoners – many of which are now closed, or owned or sponsored by private enterprises. The lovely Whitechapel Baths (first opened in 1846, blitzed in November 1944, reopened in 1962) were finally closed in 1990 by the Liberal-Democrat-controlled borough of Tower Hamlets. They included a popular swimming pool, used by four thousand schoolchildren each month, as well as slipper baths for one of London's poorest communities. Some of the older regulars, like Barnet Markovitch and Frederick Miller, neither of whom had a bathroom at home, told me they had been going there for sixty years. The lido in Brockwell Park is one survivor, but only thanks to a mineral-water company which has painted an outsize logo on the pool's floor and renamed it the Evian Lido. And Turkish baths – among which were the glamorous

Savoy baths in Jermyn Street (you can still see the sign set into the pavement) where the spy Guy Burgess used to like to hang out – are restricted today to those at Ironmonger Row and the Porchester Baths.

By the outbreak of the Second World War, the LCC had built a total of 86,000 new homes across Greater London. And while the style was changing – the estates of rather soulless neo-Georgian cottages in outlying areas like Becontree Heath on the outskirts of Dagenham, for instance – the intent was still good: soundly constructed, affordable housing for many of London's key workers.

Much of this changed during the 1950s, '60s and '70s, when all sorts of mistakes were made in the planning, design, construction and management of new council housing. Most of the problems can be put down to haste. Haste and the ambition and vanity of politicians. Why? After VE and VJ Days in 1945, successive governments promised to build 300,000 new houses a year throughout the country. This was an ambitious figure, and led to a search for fast, new, factory-style techniques. Politicians smiled and shared jokes with architects and residents for the cameras as the new concrete estates were raced up. But the skills and technology needed to make decent mass-produced houses were clearly in their infancy, and the result was a considerable amount of inept housing. The collapse of one whole corner of the Ronan Point tower block in 1968 after a gas explosion in one of the kitchens was proof not so much that high-rise was inherently dangerous (it isn't) but that Brits weren't very good at building into the sky. We liked to try and do it on the cheap, and that just can't be done.

By the early 1980s, councils had all but abandoned responsibility for new housing. This was not entirely a decision of their own making. By the time Mrs Thatcher and her privatisation-or-bust government were installed in 1979, the spending powers of local authorities were being capped. And then, at first slowly and then suddenly, in an unseemly and ultimately criminal rush, council homes were sold off at low prices. This was partly to reduce the responsibility and thus the financial burden of London's housing stock on local authorities and the public purse, and partly to encourage working-class votes away from the Labour party. It was a gloriously seedy moment for London when Dame Shirley Porter, Tory leader of Westminster Council and the daughter of Jack Cohen, founder of the Tesco supermarket chain, was found guilty in court of illegally selling houses for votes. This week's special offer. Hurry, while stocks last. You couldn't have made it up, as Londoners like to say.

So, there we were in the Eighties, Broadgate bludgeoning its way into the City and Canary Wharf on the horizon. Brash boys in their startlingly bright red braces and big-haired girls in power suits earning barrow-loads of money in the banks. Suspect developers buying up shabby old houses, dividing them up into wobbly flats and selling them off to eager young professionals. At the same time, everything public that could be sold was being sold. The government would have privatised pavements, the air we breathe, parliament itself if it could have. In a neat and spiteful move, it shut down the GLC in 1986, making London the only capital city in the world without its own governing body, and then sold the GLC's former home, County Hall, to developers to convert into private flats, a hotel and a giant aquarium. Very fishy. The price of housing shot through the roof, and councils could no longer afford, even if they'd wanted to, to build homes for those unable or unwilling to board Mrs Thatcher instant gravy train (which was, of course, about to hit the buffers as the City careered into Black Friday in 1989).

The laws of the market are rarely good ones when it comes to urban housing. Just before he died I went for a walk around Keeling House in Bethnal Green with Denys Lasdun, architect of the National Theatre. Keeling House is an imaginative block of flats built in a clover pattern by Lasdun for the LCC in the early 1950s. By the 1990s, the experimental structure needed major repairs. They weren't forthcoming, mainly because of cost, and even though the residents liked these flats – they suited the community, were well thought-out, bright and sunny and with soul-stirring views of London – they were moved out. The council eventually sold the block to a developer, who employed a good firm of architects, Munkenbeck and Marshall, to do them up. They consulted with Lasdun, and on the whole he was happy with their work. But as we poked our noses into the smart new flats and peered over the concrete balconies at the City views, we couldn't help feeling angry that these idealistic post-war council flats were no longer for the people who needed them most. They had been shifted on. Urban Gypsies. Outsiders. Not shareholders in the brutal market economy.

Housing associations like Peabody and Coin Street have more recently begun to build intelligent and popular modern city housing. A century on from the LCC's Boundary Estate, Coin Street can be proud of its most recent housing on the South Bank; so too Peabody with the fine new Murray Grove housing at Shepherdess Walk, Hackney, a modern-day interpretation of pre-fabricated housing designed by London architects Cartwright Pickard. Each steel flat was manufactured on a production line in York, complete with fixtures and fittings including kitchen, bathroom, heating, wiring, plumbing and

The development of Paddington Basin, another site likely to offer predominantly private housing (over)

carpets, and then taken on the back of a lorry to Hackney and lifted into place. It took just five days to slot the thirty-five flats together. If this all sounds a little too machine age for comfort, take heart. The flats are clad in timber, each boasts a generous balcony giving on to a communal garden, and each forms part of an architectural composition that manages to be both urban and welcoming. Murray Grove proves that London can afford intelligent, modern, attractive and low-rent housing. I like the fact that Yorkton, the company that assembled the flats, does a lot of work for fast-food chains: the lesson is that the latest technologies can be put at the service of London in ways it can really benefit from.

To build low-cost housing where it is most needed requires new strategies like this. Low-rent homes need to be built throughout central London and the suburbs, and not in big clusters or the giant estates of the past. And it should be compulsory to incorporate low-rent flats into all new private housing developments. Something else that needs doing is an audit of all the publicly owned land and property left in London. There's a lot of it – all those redundant buildings and railway yards, those scrappy bits of land that no one seems to want, that landscape of rusting cars, broken-down factories and yards full of old tyres and junk – and it needs to be reclaimed, managed and put to use in the best way possible for the long-term future of all Londoners. This may ultimately mean the GLA becoming something of a developer itself. If it, or some other publicly accountable body, can raise bonds to finance new property acquisitions and building works then London may start getting the affordable new homes for rent it so urgently needs. Then we may find that the land we hold in common, whether it's the playground of Pimlico School or the old bus works, can't simply be flogged off to the private sector and then mortgaged back to us a few years down the line.

Murray Grove, Hackney

CIRCUS No. 6

Sponsored by British Airways, the London Eye is the world's sleekest big wheel. It is the least pretentious of the Lottery-funded Millennium projects and its purpose is simple, to enchant its millions of queuing visitors with peerless views over the capital. From the top, the entire London basin can be seen – a breathtaking sight at sunset, as street and office lights are switched on. The wheel was designed and championed by the architects Marks Barfield. It was built over the surface of the Thames and then raised, dramatically, into

place. At first, it looked as if it might throw a wobbly, like the Millennium Bridge downriver, but to date it has turned around smoothly and safely. A curious sight on the central London skyline, its ethereal structure does not intrude in the way that contemporary French critics felt the Eiffel Tower did when it opened in 1889. It has, however, been described as a symbol of contemporary British political culture: going round and round uselessly, getting nowhere and for no gain. This rather misses the point, as the big wheel offers millions of people a chance not just to see the sights, but to understand the ways in which London has grown and sprawled. It enables riders to see the city in the way architects and planners all too often do, standing above a map making sweeping plans for whole areas rather than walking and experiencing streets down on the ground.

TUTTI FRUTTI ON POULTRY

I f London were a country in its own right it would have a national income greater than Russia's. Yes, London is richer than the country that spreads from the Polish to the Alaskan borders and from the Arctic Circle to the Black Sea. Its dynamic economy subsidises the rest of Britain. In 1999/2000, the capital contributed £60 billion to public-sector revenues and, in return, received £47 billion from government spending. London imports £89 billion (1998 figure) of goods and services from elsewhere in the UK, supporting 4.7 million jobs outside the capital.

Londoners – one in eight of all Britons – are paid, on average, more than 30 per cent above the national average, but this is a figure drawn from a huge range which sees subsistence-wage workers at one end and the highest paid executives in Europe at the other. The cost of living is something like 13 per cent higher than in the rest of the country, which means that many of its less-well-paid workers – up to a half of the city's population – are now unable to afford to buy a home. Despite this, London's population has been growing rapidly over the past decade (5.7 per cent between 1991 and 1998 compared with 2.9 per cent nationally). Bigger than that of Scotland, in 2000 it exceeded the combined populations of Birmingham, Blackpool, Bradford, Bristol, Derby, Glasgow, Kirklees, Leeds, Leicester, Liverpool, Manchester, Northampton, Oldham, Plymouth, Sheffield and Wolverhampton. This population is, on average, younger than that of the rest of Britain (36 compared with 38.2 years) and much less likely to work in manufacturing (11 per cent compared with a national average of 20 per cent) than in business services (one in four jobs in London). The public sector is, predictably, weaker in London than in the rest of the country, accounting for 14.5 per cent of the capital's income compared with a national average of 17.5 per cent.

What we have here is a picture of a wealthy yet imbalanced economy. An income that could buy Russia is so unevenly distributed that it includes at one end of the spectrum an ever-increasing number of very wealthy people who can afford to dress up in expensive clothes to attend the champagne-and-canapé launches of charities dedicated to things like the ending of Third World Debt. At the other end are women and children thin through no choice of their own toiling in sweatshops in boroughs where TB and rickets are rife and in conditions no better than those found in many parts of that same debt-laden Third World.

Some of the poorest wards of Britain and the nastiest sweatshops in Europe are to be found in the shadows of the towers of the City of London, that air-conditioned showcase of deregulated, free-market economics. I have a view of the City from my balcony at home. To my left is Tower 24, the former NatWest Tower (1980) designed by Colonel Seifert that rises in the guise of a 600-feet-tall NatWest logo. (The Tower has a bar at the top where you have to book a seat to have a drink.) Then there's the Bladerunner-like Lloyd's building (1986) by the Richard Rogers Partnership; the padded-shouldered post-Modernism of Terry Farrell's Alban Gate (1987) straddling London Wall; a new speculative office on Wood Street (2000) by the Rogers team (again); the dome of St Paul's (1710) and the 440-feet-tall bush-hammered concrete sculpture of the Barbican's Lauderdale Tower (1972).

Down below is the medieval church of St Giles-without-Cripplegate last rebuilt in the 1950s by Godfrey Allen. Oliver Cromwell was married here and John Milton is buried in its grounds. In 1793, Milton's corpse was exhumed. Elizabeth Grant, the care-

Tower 42

taker, charged the public sixpence a gawp. She later reduced this to threepence and then tuppence, market forces being what they were, and anyway one spectator had already given Milton's skull a good whack with a stone to loosen his teeth so he could sell them as souvenirs. A case of damaged goods then, and so hardly worth sixpence which at the time would have bought a poor person four meals of broth and bread in a London soup kitchen, paid the average working man's rent for half the week or bought a rake a quick one-up against an alley wall with a young harlot.

This was the John Milton, by the way, one of our greatest poets. Yes, yes, but the City, the cradle of London, and still, for me, its heart, has never been anything other than a rough and ready place. Anything and everything here has pretty much always been up for sale. Want to make a crust? Why not dig up John Milton's corpse and show it about a bit? And just look at those buildings dominating the view from my balcony. Banks, trading houses, money markets and the great civic temple of St Paul's, around which the City still turns and around which a whole new generation of flashy new machines for making money is being built. It was the City, you remember, that didn't want Wren's handsome new street plan after the Great Fire of 1666. No offence, of course; the City just wanted to get its hands back in the greasy till as quickly as possible.

Where there's money to be made, there's no time to lose on niceties. Even St Paul's was paid for grudgingly, largely through a tax on coal. The City might have shed a few crocodile tears over the loss down the years of well over half of Wren's famous City churches rebuilt after the Great Fire. But as recently as the 1930s Harold Clunn, author of The Face of London and unstinting champion of grandiloquent new commercial palaces, called for the demolition of St Mary Woolnoth, one of the finest creations of the English Baroque.

Lloyd's of London

Designed by Nicholas Hawksmoor, this haunting church stands like some pugnacious guard dog protecting the path to God in a labyrinth of streets dedicated first and foremost to Mammon. Clunn's case for demolition was twofold: first, St Mary's was out of scale with the imposing new banks and counting houses; second, it occupied valuable land that could be earning the City a better return than God.

The church still stands. The City, however, a largely self-governing anomoly, remains squeezed into its world-famous square mile and so will always complain that it has no room to expand. In fact it always has expanded, its buildings growing ever taller and more corpulent over the centuries and, in the case of Alban Gate, spanning a dual-carriageway to gain extra accommodation. In the 1980s, the City found space for the mighty Broadgate development, all brass, marble, ambitious public art and almighty cheek. Now it wants to build a new generation of skyscrapers, including Norman Foster's inventive, gherkin-shaped Swiss-Re headquarters on the site of the old Baltic Exchange blown up by the IRA in 1997. It is beginning to build a march of high-stepping offices north along Broadgate and, despite popular and critical opposition, wants to redevelop Spitalfields Market with more shiny stuff.

The City exists, and this has long been its great strength, not to serve the Crown, government, parliament or other vested interests, but to make money for its own ends. London was always separate from the seat of the Crown at Westminster and, like other European cities, it received its charters of independence in the early twelfth century; its constitution, ratified by King John's Magna Carta signed at Runnymede on the banks of the Thames in 1215, was based on that of Rouen.

With two thousand years of largely uninterrupted money-making experience at its fingertips – running from the Romans dealing at the Exchange to the powerful trade guilds established around Cheapside in medieval times, to the current dizzy fortunes generated daily – it is the City's wealth which has kept it mostly immune from political change. Possessed of a municipal authority all of its own, the Corporation of London, it is literally a world apart from the rest of Britain. And now, in grim echo of its centuries-old Roman wall, the City has a new electronic border in the form of the Ring of Steel. Erected after the 1997 IRA bomb, this is a series of road blocks around the City, guarded by police officers and CCTV cameras (of which London, as a whole, boasts more than any city in the world) which film and check within four seconds the registration of every vehicle entering the City.

Because of its almost exclusive devotion to the business of money and trade, the City has long been populated, and much of it owned, by enterprising foreigners. The bank of Rothschild, which is the official gold broker to the Bank of England, fixing the metal's world price every day at noon, has as its founding father Nathan Meyer Rothschild. He hailed from Frankfurt originally, but settled in England in 1798 building up a textile export business in Manchester before coming to London in 1811 to make a fortune dealing and contracting for government loans during the Napoleonic wars. Peter Palumbo, the property developer who tried for years to build a Mies van der Rohe-designed office tower opposite George Dance's eighteenth-century Mansion House (official home of the Lord Mayor of London), but instead put up the big post-Modern confection by James Stirling and Michael Wilford known as No.1 Poultry, is a well known City figure. What a dash he cuts in his immaculate, bespoke suits. What a patron of the arts. What a gent. His grandfather came to the City from Naples and sold ice-cream on its streets. Come to think of it, No.1 Poultry does look a bit like a large portion of tutti frutti. London loves money and pretty much anyone – *tutti* as the Italians say – who learns how to make it. Today, in keeping with its global-financial-powerhouse image, London's banking community is drawn from pretty much everywhere.

How wealthy is the City? Almost as wealthy as Nigeria, in fact. Its contribution to gross domestic product in 2000 was estimated to have been £168.6 billion (equivalent to 21 per cent of the UK's total economic activity). Office space here is worth up to £1,000 a square foot, which gives some indication of the wealth of the corporations renting it. The City's share of the global foreign-exchange market is 32.3 per cent, nearly twice that of the US (Tokyo, in third place, has 7.5 per cent), and it has 58 per cent of the global foreign-equity

Griffins marking entrances to the City's square mile at Temple (left) and Fleet Street (right)

market. It controls 29 per cent of the world's aviation insurance and 22 per cent of the marine insurance market. It is the largest centre for institutional equity management in the world and is the major supplier of capital to the global economy. In its own words, the City "lubricates the world".

The rest of the world likes the City because it is openly competitive, and clean, both commercially and physically (it won Britain's cleanest city award last year). There are 108 full operating subsidiaries of banks from the European Union here, employing approximately 31,000 staff. Nearly half of Europe's financial business is conducted in London. Altogether the City employs more than 300,000 people in the financial services industry, with a further 580,000 in supporting professions and an even greater number in the service industries contracted to clean, cook, drive, serve, dress-

Crowds at Liverpool Street station on a Friday evening

make, hair-dress, manicure, holiday-book … London's financial sector as a whole makes a significant contribution to Britain's gross national product, which is one reason why governments of left, right and centre have, for better or worse, tended to leave it alone to get on with the business of making money.

Compare this hands-off but nurturing approach with what's happened in another part of London where a solid manufacturing base has been allowed to disappear. The Lea Valley was home for decades to many of Britain's most innovative companies. The first all-British airplane, designed by Alliott Verdon Roe (1877–1958), flew from Walthamstow Marshes on the 13th of July 1909. It was powered by a 9hp JAP engine, made by John Alfred Prestwick (1874–1952) at his factory in Tottenham. A.V. Roe (Avro) went on to produce the Lancaster, one of very best Second World War bombers. Avro-Lancasters were equipped with Browning .303 machine-guns, but the British troops they flew over on their way to destroy German cities were weighed down with the Lee-Enfield rifles we knew so well as schoolchildren. These were first designed in 1895 by James Lee Paris, a Scot who emigrated to Canada and then to the US, and were manufactured at the Royal Small Arms Works at Enfield Lock. William Congreve's rocket factory, where the first British military rockets (employed during the Napoleonic Wars) were manufactured, was at Bromley-by-Bow. The crossed hammers of West Ham FC refer to working methods at the old Thames Ironworks at Bow Creek which built battleships (HMS Thunderer was the last in 1911). The first standard London bus, the B-Type (designed and built for the London General Omnibus Company), was produced at the LGOC's subsidiary AEC at Tottenham in 1910. Production by March 1913 was

Stratford station, an important link between the Lea Valley and the City (over)

fifty buses a week, by which time there were two thousand B-Types on the London roads. For every 100,000 miles these open-topped double-deckers travelled, they made only fourteen unscheduled stops caused by mechanical defect. It was a proud record for AEC, the LGOC (incorporated into the LPTB in July 1933) and the Lea Valley.

AEC moved to Southall in the 1930s where it crafted generations of peerless London buses, the last of which, the RML, ended production in 1968. Today, industrial nous seems so discouraged that it's hard to imagine a bus being made, much less a large aircraft or ship. The factories of the Lea Valley, however, were a showcase of London's inventive light industries, scientific knowledge and craft skills, most of which were of course lost in the 1970s and '80s when Britain's governments, determined to undermine the last vestiges of working-class power and to replace factories with supermarkets, gave up the industrial ghost and sent the population on a gigantic bread-and-circuses shopping spree instead.

The end result for the Lea Valley is an area deprived and crying out for intelligent redevelopment. This is not beyond the bounds of possibility; the river Lea, after all, is a natural link between the City (via the forthcoming rail link to Stratford), continental Europe (Stratford's Eurostar station) and the "enterprising towns" of Essex and Cambridgeshire. A revived Lea Valley might prompt a return to some of the industrial expertise of old – building some future generation of purpose-designed buses for a newly integrated London Transport, for instance. But any upturn in its fortunes is going to require a turnaround from the thinking that enables the City to be liberated from the constraints to which most of the rest of the economy is in hock.

The divide between the City and what was manufacturing industry has been cultural and political as well as economic.

London's workforce needs to be reskilled from top to bottom. This, of course, may mean an educated workforce that thought carefully about politics again – a frightening proposition for politicians who have grown used to burger-servers and check-out assistants who can be paid peanuts and kept in the apolitical dark.

From the top of the bar in Tower 42, you can't quite see to Russia, and you can't really see Spitalfields below you, but you can see across to the dark, winding ribbon of the Lea Valley. Fingers crossed that it doesn't light up with yet more finance industry guff, but becomes the home of new skills and new, ground-up intelligence in twenty-first-century London.

CIRCUS No. 7

When the notoriously insular City finally poked its proboscis out into the world with the construction of the pedestrian-only Millennium Bridge, it all seemed to go horribly wrong. The design of the bridge, a radical reworking of the classic twentieth-century suspension bridge, was anything but pedestrian. It combined the long-tried-and-tested skills of the structural engineers Ove Arup and Partners, the architects Foster and Partners and the sculptor Anthony Caro. It looked wonderful and was a lovely gesture, connecting the City's great civic

temple, St Paul's, with Southwark's new temple of art for all, Tate Modern. It linked north and south London and connected the City, richer even than old Croesus, with one of the country's poorest boroughs. Famously, it wobbled. On the day of its opening in May 2000, a huge crowd set the bridge swaying. It was safe, but induced sea-sickness. If the rough, spirited Thames could have smiled that day, it would have surely been with a wicked grin. The bridge was immediately closed as the question of how to tame it was discussed. For a while longer, at least, the City seemed as far away from Southwark as ever before. The good news, however, is that dampers have since been installed below the bridge's walkway to keep its sway in check, rather as if Marilyn Monroe had been packed off to the Lucy Clayton school to learn how to walk primly and properly. The bridge was due to re-open at the end of 2001.

HOT
AIR
AND GREAT
STINKS

A week in politics, said Harold Wilson, is a long time. So Ken Livingstone can be forgiven for saying he thought the idea of a mayor for London was a daft one shortly before he stood for the post. The turnout on the day, 4th of May 2000, was a rather apathetic 38 per cent. Perhaps a new design of trainer had just hit Oxford Street, or there was an all-day re-run of Big Brother on the telly. Whatever, the majority of Londoners couldn't be bothered to vote, despite not having had a London government to represent them for fourteen years.

Yet who can blame them for their casual attitude to the mayoral election? They knew the result was a foregone conclusion, although, astonishingly, the government really did seem to think it could beat Ken Livingstone with Frank Dobson. For better or worse, Livingstone is a Londoner's Londoner. It's not hard to imagine him driving a number 6 bus, working a stall on East Street Market or a porter's shift in St Thomas's Hospital. Sharp as a switchblade, Livingstone is London's Everyman. The fact that he had no rival is both funny and sad.

Dobson was dead in the water as far as most Londoners were concerned. A government stooge, the more he protested he wasn't, the more potential votes he lost. Norris was the former car salesman who didn't like sitting next to smelly commuters, but as most Londoners are commuters and do their best not to smell despite stifling conditions, big Steve stank. And, who could forgive the Tories (who?) for thinking for a moment that Jeffrey Archer ought to be considered? Perhaps the Kray brothers, if they'd been around, would have voted for him; or that trader who went down for a con job in the City but then got a dose of Alzheimers … can't for the life of me remember his name. The Lib-Dem candidate? I can't remember her name either.

Perhaps the truth is that the government knew it could wield a double-edged sword in these cavalier elections. If their man won, then the GLA would be neatly sewn into New Labour's pocket. If he lost and Livingstone won, then the mayor's powers would be so limited as to rob little power from central government. For all the talk of how important a mayor and a democratic city government were in the lead-up to the general election of 1997, the mayoral election proved to be a cynical exercise.

London has always, except between 1986 and 2000, had its own government of one form or other. Its size, complexity and wealth mean that, in terms of day-to-day issues, it needs to be able to govern itself. Moreover, much of the best of the city's infrastructure was established under the auspices of successful local governance: London's main sewers, for example, were built under the direction of Joseph Bazalgette, chief engineer of the Metropolitan Board of Works. Mind you, the job was only done because of the Great Stink of 1858, which meant that the windows of the Palace of Westminster had to be draped with curtains soaked in chloride of lime to mitigate the disgusting smell. The stink came from the Thames, an open sewer for all the city's effluence after a law was passed in 1847 banning domestic cesspits. No longer did salmon leap along the Thames as they had done at the beginning of the century (they returned in 1974). The river was effectively dead. And dangerous. Cholera epidemics broke out soon afterwards. As soon as MPs were directly affected, action was taken. By 1875, Bazalgette had built the 1,300 miles of sewers and the romantic pumping stations that we still rely on in 2001. Since Bazalgette, we have had a lot of hot air wafting over Westminster but no great stinks (unless you count the Archer or Profumo affairs). And cholera died out.

The LCC was established in 1889 and led from 1934 by Herbert Morrison, Peter Mandelson's grandfather. Morrison was one of London's most effective political leaders and he made the LCC a formidable body. Ostensibly its job was to sort out the sewers and drains and such like, but Morrison and his democratically elected cohorts saw their chance to remodel London along the lines of the powerful, energetic and radical city-state it was becoming. Within its boundaries, the LCC also set about creating a forerunner of the welfare state. London, whatever happened at Westminster, was to become a model of what Frank Pick, as chief executive of the LPTB, called "democratic order". In other words, London would get transport, health and education systems that worked. These required fairly heavy-handed measures to get them going, but they were generally successful and their executives were always democratically accountable through the LCC. From 1934, the LCC was a Labour hegemony (it was Labour controlled until its replacement by the GLC in 1965); it was also, by and large, extremely effective.

It was also able, unlike the GLC which ultimately lost control, to extend its powers through successive acts of parliament. At the time of the height of its power – 1930s to 1960s – it was responsible for the guts of London's infrastructure – its fire service, its building methods and housing, along with the formidably efficient LPTB. It also rebuilt bridges and tunnels (Blackwall, Rotherhithe), new roads and city streets like Kingsway, complete with its underpass for trams, and introduced planning controls to stop the spread of the city and to curb the worst kind of development. In 1938, it created the Green Belt, intended to be a sacrosanct ring of parks, woods, forests and farms around the capital to stop London merging into a great extra-urban blur with the towns and, later, the new towns beyond it. It educated London's schoolchildren with conspicuous success. It ran health authorities and the public-assistance programmes that gave relief to the city's poor.

Within its fiefdom, individual boroughs were able to push their own political agendas to left or right. Finsbury, perhaps the most radical, and certainly one of the poorest boroughs (it was merged with Islington in 1965), pushed ahead with a modern housing and health programme that earned it the tag the Peoples' Republic of Finsbury, especially after it elected Communist councillors. A stone-the-crows' throw from the chic new restaurants on Exmouth Market, you can find the Finsbury Health Centre. Designed by the Georgian émigré Berthold Lubetkin, who had witnessed the October Revolution while a student in Moscow, here was a remarkable outpost of Soviet thinking and neo-Constructivist architecture in a part of central London wracked with rickets and TB.

Nearby (opposite the newly rebuilt Sadler's Wells Theatre, the first of London's Millennium Lottery projects) are some of London's finest council flats, notably the Spa Green Estate. Lubetkin designed Spa Green's snaking blocks in 1938, but construction was delayed because of the war until 1946–49. They were built to an exacting standard – Lubetkin had previously designed the fine Highpoint I and II apartment blocks for private buyers at Highgate – and featured such novel considerations as rubbish chutes and an aerofoil roof designed to help clothes' drying on Mondays (washing day). They were expensive, but dignified. Some years later, in trying to design to a very high and humane standard for miners at Peterlee New Town in County Durham, the exacting Lubetkin fell out with his clients and abandoned his profession, though he was later awarded the Roya Gold Medal for Architecture. When he was in his eighties, I used to go down to see him at his Regency cottage in Clifton near Brunel's famous suspension bridge. He cooked Georgian stews and could

Lubetkin's Finsbury Health Centre

easily drink a young visitor under the table. He spent evenings at a casino in Bristol in the company of women sixty years his junior, and won. Other visitors used to tell me about the evacuated animals the Lubetkins cared for during the war – Lubetkin's first major commissions had been for London Zoo, and included the poetic Penguin Pool. There were even tales of a chimpanzee driving a tractor. Lubetkin was one of a number of Russian and eastern European emigres, mostly Jewish, who came to London in the 1930s. Erich Mendelsohn, the great Prussian architect, was another – his Shocken department store in Chemnitz (later Karl Marx Stadt in the German Democratic Republic) was the inspiration behind William Crabtree's sinuous steel and glass Peter Jones store on Sloane Square. Another was the Hungarian Ernö Goldfinger, who befriended the thriller writer Ian Fleming and gave his name to Fleming's best-known Bond villain (the architect's thick, guttural voice was also borrowed for the film version of Goldfinger). Goldfinger designed the Brutalist high-rise Trellick Tower which overlooks the Grand Union Canal on Golborne Road in Portobello. At the dark heart of a poverty-stricken "sink estate", Trellick Tower almost inevitably became fashionable in the early 1990s. Since then, Goldfinger's offices for Sanderson Wallpapers on Berners Street, W1, have been given the Ian Schrager–Philippe Starck treatment and transformed into the sleek and shiny Sanderson Hotel.

Back in 1940s' Finsbury, the Peoples' Republic erected a monument to Lenin. This led to protest at local and national level. Although not as heated as it might have been – Uncle Jo (Stalin) had after all been our ally against Hitler's Germany from 1941 to 1945 – the monument was seen as too alien and eventually it had to go.

Winston Churchill got revenge of sorts on London's lefties, not once, but twice, in two separate administrations. The first was during

The monument to Lenin in Finsbury

the Second World War when he personally banned one of the posters Abram Games designed in 1943 as part of the "It's your war, fight for it now" campaign. It showed Lubektin's health centre emerging from the ruins of a slum-infested London in which you can make out the figure of an emaciated boy with rickets. This infuriated Churchill, who took the opportunity to stub out his cigar, as it were, on the socialist ambitions of Finsbury. Yet sympathy was ultimately on the little poster boy's side: Churchill was swept from office in 1945 as a Labour government of all talents under Major Attlee took office. The direction it would take was made clear by the appointment of Herbert Morrison as deputy prime minister. London had been the testbed of the welfare state; now its policies would be adopted on a national scale.

Labour didn't last long though. Churchill was returned to office as prime minister of a Conservative government in 1951 and one of the first things he did was to order the demolition of the Festival of Britain buildings. Down they came, Ralph Tubbs's flying-saucer-like Dome of Discovery, demolished according to a contemporary Movietone newsreel to "add to the stocks of the country's scrap metal". (Churchill would have enjoyed that line.) Down came the Skylon, a gloriously ethereal steel and aluminium needle designed by the young architects Powell and Moya, who went on to build the successful Churchill Gardens council-housing scheme across the Thames from Battersea Power Station, which provided heating for the well-designed flats. Only the Royal Festival Hall stayed. The Festival had been one of the high points of Morrison's career – something that can't be said of his grandson's efforts with the Millennium Experience at the other Dome – and a high point, too, for LCC London.

In today's terms, the LCC might be considered paternalistic, but it can't be denied that it did a great deal both for London and, from

1945, for Britain generally – its whole-hearted experiments in free
universal education and advanced health care informed the Education
Act of 1944 and the National Heath Service created in 1948. Politics,
naturally, are never a neat and tidy business, and the LCC's "new
order" did suffer occasional disruptions. One such was the pitched
battle fought between local residents, siding with left-wing protesters, and the police in Cable Street, E1, on the 5th of October 1936
while the police were guiding Oswald Mosley's fascist Blackshirts
through the East End to Westminster. The march was finally stopped,
although during the following week, in the spirit of the Nazi's
Kristallnacht, the windows of every Jewish shop along the Mile End
Road were smashed. Trades' unions were also powerful throughout
the life of the LCC, as befitted a democratic order, and actions like the
1958 busmans' strike momentarily threatened to drag the capital to a
halt (although pea-souper fogs could be just as effective). But generally things ran smoothly enough, and in any case this was an era
when political debate was part and parcel of everyday life.

Problems in the governing of London didn't get serious until the
1980s, when the GLC became too much of a thorn in the side of the
Thatcher government. "Radical" and "left-wing" actions on the part
of the GLC, like erecting a statue to Nelson Mandela on the west wall
of the Royal Festival Hall and inviting Gerry Adams to County Hall,
were in Margaret Thatcher's eyes indicative of a wish to be involved
in issues related more to national than local politics. Effectively, this
made the GLC a far more useful opposition than the parliamentary
Labour party. Thatcher hated it, and the GLC was eventually abolished
in 1986. History has of course since had its say – not only has Ken
Livingstone been endorsed as London's favourite mayoral candidate,

he has also been proved right in backing Mandela and encouraging a positive dialogue with Sinn Fein and the IRA. It is fair to say though that, had Livingstone stuck to London issues in the 1980s, the GLC might have survived. The duty of local government is first and foremost one of drains, sewers, buses, trains, schools and hospitals. These things may not seem as exciting as international politics, but they can be. Livingstone should have, and probably has since, taken a leaf out of Herbert Morrison's book.

Not that Livingstone as mayor has anything like the power that Morrison as leader of the LCC had. Unlike his counterparts elsewhere in Europe and the US, he has no real tax-gathering or other powers that could enable him to make a real go of changing the face of London. Such impotence is symptomatic of the impulse of national government – it wants to meddle, especially where the interests of big business are concerned, but not take responsibility. Perhaps the very nature of parliament, with its MPs representing constituencies the length and breadth of Britain, precludes any real interest in London's welfare. For whatever reasons, national politicians have rarely had the vision or even the desire to improve the capital; they have rather tended to see it as something they can exploit for their own ends, a place to conduct their sexual affairs and a giant stepping stone to reach the apex of their boundless ambition.

The height of government meddling was reached in July 2001, when Tony Blair sacked Bob Kiley, the former New York Subway boss who Blair had himself appointed to sort out the London Underground. Kiley arrived in 2000 and was widely welcomed, but he made (as far as Blair was concerned) two crucial mistakes: first, he endeared himself to the mayor and, second, he disagreed with the government's vindictive scheme to part-privatise the Underground. Blair's toying with London's future in this high-handed manner was an astonishing display of arrogance. Ignorance, too. London doesn't need the government to tell it how to run the Underground. It would, in fact, be much better if the government offered advice on a generous scale and asked the mayor, the GLA and London's boroughs why on earth plans aren't already afoot to make a revitalised Underground part of a modern-day version of a fully integrated London Transport.

One small thing the GLA does have the power to do is to encourage Londoners to participate in debate, while, wherever possible, showing by example how London can be both a dynamic and a socially responsible city. The Architecture Foundation debates sponsored by the *Evening Standard* and held under the galumphing great Edwardian Baroque dome of Central Methodist Hall, Westminster were an example of just such an approach. The level of debate was high and Londoners got to talk face to face not just with those running the city, or even those who would like to run the city, but with the likes of Pasqual Maragall, the former socialist mayor of Barcelona, who has done so much to revive that charismatic city's fortunes and standing in the world.

Comparisons with other cities can seem invidious, but they're hard to avoid in an age of easy travel and global exchange. We have every right to ask why London can't have a public transport system as efficient as New York's or Moscow's. Why we're encouraged to take so little interest in public design, unlike the citizens of Barcelona or Rome. Why London's health-care system is stretched to breaking point when this isn't true of Paris. Or why our streets are generally so filthy compared with those of many European cities. Yes, London is bigger and messier by nature than many other cities, but that doesn't mean it can't learn something from them. It also needs to hear politicians admit to making mistakes. To say, yes, the Dome was a cock-up; yes, PPP is entirely the wrong way to set about improving the Underground and, no, central government shouldn't be trying to run London. London can run itself, thanks all the same. "Fear of making mistakes", Frank Pick told his staff, "is a deadly fear. To be able to be wrong is to be creative." London must be allowed to make its own mistakes.

CIRCUS No. 8

Two new millennial fortresses for politicians, London and national. Portcullis House is the big, lumpen building capped with tall, light-absorbing chimneys facing Westminster Palace across streams of traffic snarling over Westminster Bridge and along the Embankment. It provides secure, air-conditioned offices for members of parliament and a fancy atrium for rented fig trees. The very name, Portcullis House, evokes castles, and indeed this is where MPs, in an era of increasingly centralised and arrogant government, hide away from those declining numbers who vote

for them. The building was designed by Michael Hopkins and Partners, architects whose reputation is partly redeemed by the generous and handsome JLE Underground station that acts as the foundation of Portcullis House. Yet why would anyone set such a thuggish building against the much-loved filigree Gothic finery of Barry and Pugin's Palace of Westminster? In contrast, the GLA building, designed by Foster and Partners, sits to date in splendid isolation on a property developer's site on the south bank of the Thames between London and Tower Bridges. Although it may yet be open to the public, this helmet-shaped building has the air of a sci-fi castle; it could be the headquarters of Darth Vader. The building's shape is distinctive and it may prove to be among the more environmentally sound London office buildings, but it seems a shame that the new headquarters for the GLA should be leased from developers rather than custom-built. It makes the whole enterprise feel disturbingly temporary.

RESOURCE LIST

The arguments in favour of low-key yet purposeful, social planning advanced throughout this book are an attempt to shift London well away from New Labour's world of bread and circuses. If this is something you agree is worth doing, please make your voice heard. Don't say there's nothing you can do about it, or that you're never taken notice of. If you're passive or fatalistic, the London of corporate enterprise and ambitious politicians who serve the interest of business over and above civility will roll over you. And you'll believe the hype fed to us daily: London is expanding eastwards to make us all better off. No it isn't, it's mostly expanding westwards along the M4 corridor, from Paddington to Heathrow. The PPP (public-private partnership) scheme is the right one for the Underground. No it isn't, PPP is a dismal and unimaginative dogma and is not in your interest as a Londoner. Bart's Hospital doesn't need an Accident and Emergency Ward. Oh yes it does.

The list below covers many of the organisations mentioned in the book as well as other relevant bodies. Please write to them for information or with your views if you want to start effecting change. Or, if you want to write to me about your ideas for London, please do so c/o Verso, 6 Meard Street, London W1F 0EG, and I'll endeavour to get them heard.

THE ARCHITECTURE FOUNDATION
www.architecturefoundation.org.uk
T 020.7839.9389

CABE (COMMISSION FOR ARCHITECTURE AND THE BUILT ENVIRONMENT)
www.cabe.org.uk
T 020.7960.2400

CENTRAL LONDON PARTNERSHIP

www.c-london.co.uk

T 020.7665.1550

CORPORATION OF LONDON

www.cityoflondon.gov.uk

T 020.7332.3099

ENGLISH HERITAGE

www.english-heritage.org.uk

T 020.7973.3434

GREATER LONDON AUTHORITY

www.london.gov.uk

T 020.7983.4000

LONDON FORUM OF AMENITY AND CIVIC SOCIETIES

www.communityweb.org.uk

T 020.7250.0606

LONDON GYPSY AND TRAVELLER UNIT

(website being set up)

T 020.8533.2002

LONDON HOUSING FEDERATION

www.housing.org.uk

T 020.7278.6571

LONDON REGIONAL TRANSPORT

www.londontransport.co.uk

T 020.7222.5600

LONDON SCHOOL OF ECONOMICS AND POLITICAL SCIENCE

www.lse.ac.uk

T 020.7405.7686

LONDON TRANSPORT MUSEUM

www.ltmuseum.co.uk

T 020.7379.6344

LONDON UNDERGROUND LTD

www.thetube.com

T 020.7222.5600

NATIONAL HEALTH SERVICE

www.nhs.uk

T 020.7210.4850

OFFICE OF NATIONAL STATISTICS

www.statistics.gov.uk

T 0845.601.3034

PEABODY TRUST

www.peabody.org.uk

T 020.7928.7811

ROYAL INSTITUTE OF BRITISH ARCHITECTS

www.architecture.com

T 020.7580.5533

www.riba-london.com

T 020.7307.3688

ROYAL TOWN PLANNING INSTITUTE

www.rtpi.org.uk

T 020.7636.9107

SCHOOL WORKS

www.school-works.org.uk

T 020.7401.5333

TRANSPORT & GENERAL WORKERS UNION

www.tgwu.org.uk

T 020.7611.2500

TRANSPORT FOR LONDON

www.transportforlondon.gov.uk

T 020.7222.5600

TREES FOR LONDON

www.treesforlondon.org.uk

T 020.7587.1320

THE URBAN DESIGN ALLIANCE

www.udal.org.uk

T 020.7665.2210

FURTHER READING

Homes for a World City: The Report of the Mayor's Housing Commission,
GLA, 2001

Key Issues for Key Workers: Affordable Housing in London, GLA, 2001

The Mayor's Transport Strategy, GLA, 2001

London's Contribution to the UK Economy, Corporation of London, 2001

New Architecture for the Underground, David J Taylor, Capital Transport,
2001

London: The Biography, Peter Ackroyd, Chatto & Windus, 2001

Our Towns and Cities: The Future, Department of the Environment,
Transport & Regions, 2000

Leadville: A Biography of the A40, Edward Platt, Picador, 2000

London's Lea Valley, Jim Lewis, Phillimore, 1999

A History of London, Stephen Inwood, Macmillan, 1998

Designed for London: 150 years of Transport Design, Oliver Green and
Jeremy Rewse-Davies, Laurence King, 1995

The London Encyclopaedia, Ben Weinreb and Christopher Hibbert,
MacMillan, 1993 (revised edition)

A New London, Richard Rogers and Mark Fisher, Penguin, 1992

The Conscious of the Eye: The Design and Social Life of Cities, Richard
Sennett, Faber & Faber, 1991

Nairn's London, Ian Nairn, Penguin, 1988 (revised edition)

London 2001, Peter Hall, Unwin Hyman, 1984 (revised edition)

London: The Unique City, Steen Eiler Rasmussen, MIT Press, 1982 (new
edition)

London as it might have been, Felix Barker and Ralph Hyde, John Murray,
1982

A Revolution in London Housing: LCC Architects and Their Work, 1893-
1914, Susan Beattie, GLC and Architectural Press, 1980

The Architects of London, Alastair Service, Architectural Press, 1979

The Changing Life of London, George Gardiner, Tom Stacey, 1973

Semi-Detached London, Alan A Jackson, George Allen & Unwin, 1973

The East End of London, Millicent Rose, Cedric Chivers, 1973 (revised edition)

The City in History, Lewis Mumford, Penguin, 1961

Counter Attack Against Suburbia, Ian Nairn, Architectural Press, 1957

The Buildings of England Series: London, four volumes, ed. Nikolaus Pevsner, Penguin, from 1957

Greater London Plan 1944, Patrick Abercrombie, HMSO, 1945

London Replanned: The Royal Academy Planning Committee's Interim Report, Country Life, 1942

Britain Must Rebuild, Frank Pick, Kegan Paul (Democratic Order series), 1941

London Revived: Considerations for its Rebuilding in 1666, John Evelyn (ed. E S Beer), Clarendon Press, 1938

The Spirit of London, Paul Cohen-Portheim, Batsford, 1935

The Face of London, Harold Clunn, Simpkin, 1932

London and Westminster Improved, John Gwynn, published by the author, 1766

A Survey of London, John Stow, John Wolfe, 1598

ACKNOWLEDGEMENTS

This book would have been impossible to write without the diligent research and unfailing good nature of Helen Jones of Restructure; the enthusiasm and kindness of my editor Jane Hindle, who commissioned it; and the support of my agent, Sarah Chalfant of the Wylie Agency. Thanks to everyone who has offered advice even though I may have disagreed with it, and especially to Peter Buchanan, Ricky Burdett, Michael Cassidy, Hilary Cottam, Tim Dudderidge, Paul Finch, my colleagues at the *Guardian*, Harry Handelsman, Peter Hendy, the staff of the London Transport Museum, Vivien Lovell, Fred Manson, Roland Paoletti, Dickon Robinson, and Richard Rogers. Thanks to Mark and Gillian and Rob and Kath for places to write away from London, which is as much a distraction as an inspiration. And to Ben Weinreb and Christopher Hibbert for their peerless *London Encyclopaedia*, the Londoner's Bible.

Many thanks too to Nigel Fowler Sutton, who did the original photography for the book, and to Stuart Smith who designed it.

Other photographs were sourced as follows, and grateful acknowledgement is given for permission to use them: the *Guardian* for page 1 (May Day demonstrations 2001), photograph by Graham Turner; London Transport for pages 30 and 36–7 (Frank Pick and Stockwell Garage), photographs from London Transport Museum; the Royal Institute of British Architects for page 132 (Lenin monument); Mary Evans Picture Library for pages 134–5 (1951 Festival of Britain buildings), photograph by Gerald Wilson.